PERIL OF ISLAM

Telling the Truth!

by Gene Gurganus

Truth Publishers

Taylors, SC

PERIL *of* ISLAM

Telling the Truth!

by Gene Gurganus

Truth Publishers
Taylors, SC

TABLE OF CONTENTS

Dr. David Yearick,
Pastor Emeritus

"Of making many books there is no end." (Ecclesiastes 12:12).
Indeed many books have been written about the religion of
Islam, but as Peter said of the writings of Paul, they contain
"some things hard to understand." (II Peter 3:10). The author's
purpose in writing this book is to warn us about the dangers of
Islam in an easy-to-understand style, which can be read by the
average reader in a couple of hours. This does not mean that
the book is unworthy of serious attention. Dr. Gurganus lived
in a Muslim country for seventeen years sharing the Gospel of
Jesus Christ with thousands of people and learning much about
their religion while intermingling with them on a daily basis.
He has also diligently studied Islam for forty-five years. Therefore, his personal knowledge of his subject is most remarkable.
As you read this book, you will notice that he relies not only on
his own knowledge, but quotes liberally from other authors.

Dr. Gurganus is not a "johnny-come-lately" author, having been
used of God to write at least five other books. He is to be commended for his courage in writing the *Peril of Islam* but has
done so out of a great burden to acquaint people with the most
rapidly growing false religion in the world. Read it carefully
and read it prayerfully, and you will gain much that will enable
you *"to be ready always to give an answer to every man that asketh
you a reason of the hope that is in you"* (I Peter 3:15) and to be
well informed about the false teachings of Islam.

DEDICATION

In this dedication I wish to single out four groups of individuals.

First, I dedicate this book to those brave men and women who have given their lives as martyrs to take the message of Christ to Muslims. I know only a few of them by name, but our Heavenly Father knows them very well. In that bright tomorrow, they will cast their martyr's crown at the Savior's feet and thank Him for the privilege of preaching His love to those who hated and killed them.

Second, I dedicate this book to brave men and women who are presently taking the message of Christ to Muslims. As one who was engaged in this noble task for seventeen years, I know the difficulties, the dangers, and the disappointments. The task is hard; the obstacles are many. The joy of seeing Muslim men and women enter into the freedom of Christ makes the task eminently worth all the difficulties.

Third, I dedicate this book to brave men and women who dare to write the truth about Islam. Their writings expose them to the hatred of those who fear the truth. I am deeply grateful to them. From their research and observations I have learned much. I cannot mention all of them but I would like to mention a few that have been most helpful to me: Daniel Pipes for his book, *Militant Islam Reaches America;* Serge Trifkovic, *The Sword of the Prophet: Islam history, theology, impact on the world;* Steve Emerson, *American Jihad; The Terrorist Living Among Us;* Eugene and Emir Caner, *Unveiling Islam, An Insider's Look at Muslim Life and Beliefs;* Robert Morey, *Islamic Invasion; Confronting the World's Fastest Growing Religion;* Mark Gabriel, *Islam and Terrorism: What the Quran Really Teaches About Christianity, Violence and the Goals of the Islamic Jihad and Islam and the Jews; The Unfinished Battle;* Ravi Zacharias, *Light in the Shadow of Jihad; The Struggle for Truth;* Norman Geisler and Abdul Saleeb, *Answering Islam; The Crescent in the Light of the Cross;* Bernard Lewis, *The Crisis of Islam; Holy War and Unholy Terror;* Don Richardson, *The Secrets of the Koran,* and Robert Spencer, *Islam Unveiled—Disturbing Questions about the World's Fastest Growing Religion.* Without these authors and their literary labors, I would not have been able to write *Peril of Islam; Telling the Truth.* May the Lord bless them and protect them.

Fourth and last, I dedicate this book to a Muslim family that turned to Christ through the testimonies and preaching of faithful missionaries. Mr. S. and Mrs. A believed in Christ, were baptized, and joined a local Baptist church. In spite of continual threats and harassment, they lived for Christ in a Muslim village and raised their children to love and serve Christ. Their son is a pastor evangelist and their daughter is married to an evangelist. This family's courage and faithfulness to Christ and His Church for the past forty years defies description.

ACKNOWLEDGMENTS

A great man once said, "When gratitude dies on the altar of a man's heart, that man is well nigh hopeless." Well, there is hope for me because I am grateful for those who helped me and encouraged me in writing this book.

First, I want to thank my editors, Bob Franklin and Bob Nestor for helping me in many ways to see this book come to birth.

Second, I want to thank Sherman Dye, master printer and faithful Christian, for enabling me to print and publish this book. Graphic artist Timm Artus is responsible for the beautiful cover.

Third, I want to thank several close friends and family members who have read each chapter as I have completed it. Their encouragement was a source of strength and joy.

Fourth, I want to thank David Yearick, my pastor of many years, for writing the foreword. Receiving his blessing upon this endeavor was important to me.

Fifth, I want to thank my God—Father, Son and Holy Spirit—for leading me to write this book and giving me the strength and wisdom to see it published.

I hope that everyone who reads this book will take time to read the preface. Anyone daring enough to write on such a controversial subject as Islam and the "clash of civilizations" can expect flack and lots of it. Muslims, of course, will accuse me of "trashing" their great religion. Most of the criticism will come from the intelligentsia and the academia joined by the liberals, both religious and political. These folks often look at things the way they wish they were and not as they really are.

For example, in spite of fourteen centuries of Islamic expansion, mostly by the use of force, still many scholars deny there is such a thing as "jihad" (holy war). To these people, anyone who dares sound an alarm concerning Islam are dismissed out of hand with derisive terms such as "islamophobe", "obscurantist", "Muslim-hater", "mud-rucker", and "trouble-maker".

The honest reader will understand that this book gives a short, abbreviated history of Islam to point out the military nature of this religion. The author goes to the source of Islam, the Koran, and quotes many surahs (chapters) to show what Muslims believe. With the help of Serge Trifkovic, Steve Emerson, Mark Gabriel, the Caner brothers, Don Richardson, and many others, I have revealed what Muslim leaders are saying about their plans for America. I choose not to be intimidated by my adversaries because I am telling the truth.

Let me say unequivocally that Islam is a great religion: a great religion for Muslims. Defenders of the Islamic faith, such as John Esposito in his massive and impressive *Oxford History of Islam,* seemingly overlook the important fact that Islam divides the world into the world of peace (Islam) and the world of war (non-Muslims). The stated goal of Islam is to bring peace to the world. To enjoy this peace, the non-Muslim world must submit to Allah and his seventh century prophet Mohammed. To me, this peace comes at too great a price. I prefer to remain a combatant.

Islamophiles look nostalgically back to the "golden age" of Islam believing that Islam holds the key to solving the multitude of problems facing our world today. My simple question to them is where is the Muslim country that has excelled in anything? Of course, the pat answer is that no Muslim country has pure Islam. The overthrow of the Shah in Iran was for the purpose of establishing a true, pure, Koranic Islamic Republic. That experiment has been the debacle of the ages, which has been a great embarrassment to Islam.

Here is just one more question for the defenders of "classical" Islam: Why have the peace-loving Muslims of the world been so quiet, so reluctant to challenge the radical, militant Muslims? If these terrorists are an aberration of Islam, why do they not publicly disassociate from them and let the world know that American Muslims do not recognize these evil men as co-religionists?

We are in a conflict to defend our faith and our way of life, the American way, the Christian way. The issue before us is not whether Muslims are good or bad, classical or radical, peaceful or militant. The critical fact that this book seeks to prove is that there are millions of people who follow the religion of Islam whose aim is to destroy the greatest democracy in history, the United States of America. The purpose of this book is to expose them. *"And have no fellowship with the unfruitful works of darkness, but rather reprove them"* (Ephesians 5:11).

Writing books is not fun; especially books that deal with life and death issues that are facing our nation. After living in a Muslim country for 17 years, studying the religion of Islam for forty-five years, recently witnessing the terrorist attacks upon our nation, and analyzing the distorted data given to the American people, this author feels an urgency to get out the truth. The media, politicians, and educators taking the politically correct route are holding down the truth. From 9/11 to the present there has been a concerted effort to separate a long series of atrocities from the religion of Islam. Remember the Muslim bombing of PanAm Flight 103! Remember the Muslim bombing of the World Trade Center in 1993! Remember the Muslim bombing of the Marine barracks in Lebanon! Remember the Muslim bombing of the military barracks in Saudi Arabia! Remember the Muslim bombing of the American Embassies in Africa! Remember the Muslim bombing of the USS COLE! Remember the Muslim attacks on the Twin Towers and the Pentagon on 9/11/2001! Remember all the American lives that were lost in those vicious Muslims attacks! The undeniable fact is that every terrorist involved in these attacks was a Muslim. Yet we are told that Islam is a religion of peace. Anyone daring to say otherwise is labeled a bigot. Franklin Graham was attacked fiercely for his truthful statement that reads as follows:

> I don't believe this is a wonderful peaceful religion when you read verses in the Koran that command the killing of infidels, i.e., those who are non-Muslims. It wasn't Methodists, it wasn't Lutherans, but it was people of the Islamic faith that flew the planes into the Twin Towers on 9/11.[1]

I do not know the crisis that motivated James Russell Cowell to pen the following words in the *Boston Courier* in 1845 but they are apropos to the days in which we live.

> Though the cause of evil prosper, yet the truth alone is strong;
> Though her portion be the scaffold, and upon the throne be wrong;
> Yet that scaffold sways the future, and behind the dim unknown, Standeth God within the shadow, keeping watch above His own.[2]

The truth does not need defending. It only needs telling. *"Ye shall know the truth and the truth shall make you free"* (John 8:32). Ravi Zacharias's observation concerning truth needs repeating:

> Most people today, when asked to define truth, stumble and stutter because they have never paused to understand what even they themselves mean when they say Jesus is "the way, the truth and the life." Truth, very simply stated, boils down to two tests: Statements made must correspond to reality, and the system of thought developed as a result must be coherent (logical and reasonable). The correspondence and coherence tests are applied by all of us in matters that affect us.[3]

In other words truth claims must be legitimately demonstrated rather than just stating it without a defense. The truth needs out and I am willing to relate as straightforward as possible the truth about the people and organizations seeking to destroy our free country. As a true patriot I cannot do otherwise. Along with James Russell Cowell we believe that "God standeth in the shadow, keeping watch over His own."

Any Muslim reading this book needs to know that we have no animosity against any person. This is not an attack upon Islam. Our purpose is not to offend or condemn rather to state the facts very clearly. It should be pointed out that Islam offends me and every true believer in Christ when it blasphemes our Lord Jesus Christ by denying His incarnation as the Son of God, His death on the cross, and His bodily resurrection from the dead. The teachings, practices, and fruit of this religious system will be set forth from their own holy books and holy men. If what their own scholars write and what trustworthy historians have written about Islam and Mohammed offends, then that is their problem. There is a plethora of information and if what they write about themselves causes them embarrassment that is not my fault. Our Lord said, *"Wherefore by their fruits ye shall know them"* (Matthew 7:20).

America is the land of the free and the home of the brave. As such we believe that every person is free to choose his or her religion. People are free to curse God and go to hell. People are free to choose their course of action but they cannot avoid the consequence of their actions. Both in the Bible and in America there is no compulsion in religion. As a Christian I have chosen to believe that Jesus Christ is the way, the truth and the life and that the Bible is the inerrant inspired Word of God. If a person chooses to trust Mohammed and believe that the Koran is the Word of Allah, I give him that privilege. However, I strongly resist any system that seeks to force me to believe it is the truth. In this nation of ours no religion which forces its tenets upon people against their wills should be given favor. In this book we will examine the facts of Islamic history, the teachings of the Koran, and the statements of Muslims leaders to discover if Islam is a religion of peace and if indeed it forces people to accept it against their wills.

My motivation in writing this book is to give the reader an easy to read, accurate but brief biography of Mohammed and history of Islam. Along with that information we seek to share concisely what Muslims believe and practice. The question of how Islam views Christians, Jews, Hindus and Buddhists will be addressed. Along that line we will discuss Roman Catholicism's recent change in policy toward Islam. Another aim is to compare the Bible and the Koran as these are the two most important and powerful books in the world. In light of the terrorist attacks upon our country and other countries around the world we will investigate what and who are behind these attacks.

Lastly, we will make some suggestions as to how we as Bible-believing Christians and patriotic American citizens should respond to the perils that threaten our republic. As a result of my research in writing this book, I feel an even greater urgency that this information be made available to the American public. My prayer is that this book will be a "wake up" call to those who love and cherish their freedom and their faith.

Gene Gurganus, 2004

End Notes:
1. Graham, Franklin, quote taken from the Presbyterian Church of America website.
2. Cowell, Russel, *Boston Courier,* 1845.
3. Zacharia, Ravi, *Living an Apologetic Life, Just Thinking,* Fall, 2003 p. 3.

Abraham is the father of three great religions: Judaism, Christianity, and Islam. All three reverence him as a prophet and a great man of God. In Genesis 12:2, 3, God gave Abraham the promise that through him and his seed all the families of the earth would be blessed. Jesus Christ, of course, is the seed of Abraham, and through Him, multitudes have been blessed; and in a coming day all the families of the earth will be blessed. The quandary plaguing today's world in the Middle East results from Abraham's inability to wait on God. This was Abraham's fatal mistake.

Year after year rolled by but Sarah, Abraham's wife bore no child. The blessing promised to Abraham depended upon a son. So Sarah took the matter in her own hands and decided to get an heir through her handmaiden, Hagar, an Egyptian. Abraham went along with the plan and in due time, a son was conceived. Tensions rose between the two women in Abraham's household, which resulted in Sarah's casting the bondwoman out into the desert.

God in His sovereignty had mercy on pregnant Hagar by sparing her life and sending her back to Abraham. At this time, God made a significant promise to Hagar and a prophecy concerning her son. *"And the angel of the LORD said unto her, Behold, thou art with child, and shalt bear a son, and shalt call his name Ishmael; because the LORD hath heard thy affliction. And he will be a wild man; his hand will be against every man, and every man's hand against him; and he shall dwell in the presence of all his brethren"* (Genesis 16:11,12). This child, Ishmael, was not the *"son of promise"* but was the son of unbelief.

Ishmael's Legacy

John Phillips in Exploring Genesis shares some interesting insights concerning Ishmael and his progeny.

> *"And he will be a wild man; his hand will be against every man, and every man's hand against him; and he shall dwell in the presence of his brethren"* (16:12). From Ishmael the Arab tribes have sprung to fulfill the role of destiny upon the stage of time

so accurately predicted of them here. They remain in the background of the Bible, joining hands with Israel's foes. They found for themselves a prophet and hurled themselves like wild men against the ramparts of the world, building up a brilliant empire and spreading their creed with the sword. Christian explorers, blazing gospel trails into Africa, found that the sons of Ishmael had gone before and had set the continent ablaze in their savage hunt for slaves. Today they sit astride the oil reserves of the world and threaten the peace of the world. Their rage against Israel keeps the world in turmoil, ever on the brink of global war. It was all foreseen and wrapped up in that embryonic prophecy spoken to Hagar long ago. What a revelation of the greatness of God wrapped up in His sovereignty![1]

In due time, God fulfilled his promise to Abraham and Sarah as a son was born to them. This son was named Isaac, a name that means "laughter". The laughter was soon erased as Ishmael, the fourteen-year-old teenager, mocked Isaac, his stepbrother. Resentment, hostility, hatred against this heir of promise boiled in Ishmael's young heart. Eventually, Sarah prevailed on Abraham to send Hagar and Ishmael away. Again God undertook for them in the desert by providing water. At this time, God made another significant prophecy concerning Ishmael.

"Arise, lift up the lad, and hold him in thine hand; for I will make him a great nation, And God opened her eyes, and she saw a well of water; and she went, and filled the bottle with water, and gave the lad drink. And God was with the lad; and he grew And dwelt in the wilderness, and became an archer. And he dwelt in the wilderness of Paran: and his mother took him a wife out of the land of Egypt (Genesis 21:18,19-21)."

In Genesis 25:12-19, we learn of Ishmael's twelve sons and of his death at the age of one hundred and thirty seven years.

Great Nation

God was true to his promise to Ishmael. Through the twelve sons of Ishmael, great nations have emerged. For the most part the histories of these nations have been blurred and lost. We do know that Arabs claim Ishmael as their father. All those who follow the prophet of Islam and the religion he established trace their heritage back to Ishmael. In the course of history, Islamic nations at one time were the centers of culture and learning, boasting such cities as Baghdad, Cairo, and Damascus. The Renaissance in the West and the military prowess of the European colonial powers severely weakened the centers of Islam. For centuries Islam was on the back burner.

In the 1920's with a growing concern about depletion of domestic oil resources, Americans became junior partners of British, Dutch, and French oil companies. In 1933, Standard Oil of America signed an agreement with King Ibn Saud.[2] The American oil companies developed the Arabian oil fields, and this oil monopoly catapulted Saudi Arabia and other Middle East countries into undreamed riches, power, and influence. These Arab oil-producing nations today have the capability of blackmailing the industrial countries of the West. Fifty years ago no one would have suspected such a resurgence of Arab power. In the meantime, their petro dollars continue to finance the Islamic advance around the world.

Ishmael or Isaac?

Ishmael is a source of conflict because the Koran states that Abraham was commanded to sacrifice Ishmael whereas the Bible states that God commanded Abraham to sacrifice Isaac. The Bible is very clear in this matter. *"And it came to pass after these things, that God did tempt Abraham, and said unto him, Abraham: and he said, Behold, here I am. And he said, Take now thy son, thine only son Isaac, whom thou lovest, and get thee into the land of Moriah; and offer him there for a burnt offering upon one of the mountains which I will tell thee of"* (Genesis 22:1-2).

Muslim Slant

Muslims insist that Abraham sacrificed Ishmael and not Isaac. How can this be when the Bible is so clear on the matter? Well, let's see how they can explain it:

> Now in reading this account you may have noticed that the boy who was going to be sacrificed is not Isaac but Ishmael, which is opposite the Biblical account of this story.
> The evidence to support this claim can be de-

rived from the Bible itself, which tells of Abraham being told to sacrifice his only son. As you well know, both Ishmael and Isaac were sons of Abraham, with Ishmael being the older, so to call Isaac his only son would be incorrect. Jewish law does not discriminate between sons born to different wives, so Muslims hold that the name Ishmael was changed to Isaac by people who had modified this ancient account. (Jewish tribal records were lost for a period of years during the Babylonian captivity and were rewritten from memory by a priest named Ezra.)[3]

What can I say? This is a case of rewriting history to make the facts fit what one wishes to be true.

Who Owns Palestine?

Another burning question concerns the subject of who owns Palestine. As far back as March 10, 1945, King Ibn Saud of Saudi Arabia wrote President Franklin Roosevelt a lengthy letter as to why the Arabs ought to be the masters of Palestine and why the Jews should be driven out. The Mohammedan King claimed that the land belonged to the Canaanites, an Arab tribe which emigrated from the Arabian peninsula as early as 3500 B.C. The king went on to blame Joshua for dislocating the Canaanites. Finally the King told President Roosevelt that the Arabs occupied Palestine in 637 A.D. and that Arab rule lasted 880 years. Then, said the King, "Palestine passed under the rule of the Turks in A.D. 1517, and their rule lasted 400 years." By whose right did the Arabs occupy Palestine in 637 A.D. and who gave the Turks the right to rule in 1517?

Dr. Noel Smith, editor of the Baptist Bible Tribune, in November of 1957 brought to light the King's letter over the question of who owns Palestine. He asked four questions that must be considered:

1. Is the book of Genesis an authentic record?
2. Did Almighty God deed and convey to Abraham and his seed, through the line of Isaac, and for an everlasting possession, all the land between the Nile and Euphrates rivers?
3. Did Almighty God have the right to do it?
4. Has Almighty God ever revoked the deed and

conveyance?[4]

The Bible speaks very plainly about who should own Palestine.

"In the same day the Lord made a covenant with Abram, saying, Unto thy seed have I given this land, from the river of Egypt unto the great river, the river Euphrates" (Genesis 15:18). Abraham's covenant seed was to be through the line of Isaac: *"And God said, Sarah thy wife shall bear thee a son indeed; and thou shalt call his name Isaac: and I will establish my covenant with him for an everlasting covenant, and with his seed after him"* (Genesis 17:19).

History of the Conflict

To properly understand the Palestinian Israeli conflict and all of its ramifications of worldwide terrorism, it is necessary for us to build on an historical foundation. This conflict is not new. The animosity between Arab and Jew is not of recent origin. It goes back to Abraham, Sarah, Hagar, Ishmael, and Isaac. As the Saudi king pointed out, the Muslims drove out the Jews in A..D. 637. However, it was the Balfour Declaration in 1917 that was pushed through the United Nations by the United States and Great Britain in 1948 that gave the displaced Jews of World War II a place to live. America's support of Israel's right to exist as a democratic sovereign country has been constant from 1948 to the present. This support for Israel causes Muslims worldwide to hate the United States. From that day in 1948 to the present, there have been constant efforts by the surrounding Muslim nations to push Israel into the sea. The strife continues and will continue.

Hopefully, pointing out these historical facts will be helpful as we deal with the subject of the peril of Islam.

End Notes:
1. Phillips,John , *Exploring Genesis,* Moody Press, Chicago, 1980, pp. 141, 142.
2. Lewis,Bernard, *The Crisis of Islam—Holy War and Unholy Terror,* The Modern Library, New York, 2003, pp. 16, 127.
3. Emerick, Yahiya, *The Complete Idiot's Guide to Understanding Islam,* Alpha Books, Indianapolis, IN, 2002, p. 154.
4. Smith, Noel, *Who Owns Palestine?—A Reply to the Arab Position,* Baptist Vision, Publication of Crown College, Powell, TN, first published in the Baptist Bible Tribune, November 29, 1957, pp. 5—7.

Take yourself back to A.D. 600. Barbarians roam the forests of Europe. The Roman Catholic Church leads its followers into centuries of darkness and oppression. Relatively speaking, the countries of India and China enjoy a higher, more developed culture. In Arabia, warring tribes prey upon one another.

Edward Gibbon, in his famous "*The Decline and Fall of the Roman Empire*" picturesquely described the country of Arabia as follows:

> The Arabian Peninsular is a vast desert area four times the size of Germany. The country is destitute of navigable rivers. The country has three distinct areas: "sandy" (desert), "stony" (mountains), and "happy" (the watered area along the Indian Ocean). There were forty-two cities: Mecca and Medina were the most famous. Two hundred seventy miles separated these cities.[1]

Character of the People

The inhabitants, the bedoween or bedouin, fierce, independent, and proud, embraced without inquiry any stranger brave enough to enter their tent with unimaginable kindness and hospitality. The women cared for the sheep and camels while the men and boys on their famous Arabian steeds practiced the art of the bow, the javelin, and the scimitar. Although they continually feuded among themselves, they would come together to defend against any outsiders who dared to attack them. Each man is free, disdaining submitting his will to a master. "Fear of dishonor guards him from the fear of pain, danger and death." The Bedouin's serious demeanor, absence of mirth, and slowness of speech was fostered, no doubt, by the harsh conditions in which he lived.[2]

The tribal-society aspect of pre-Islamic Arabia explains many of the things found in Islam today. For example, raiding caravans in order to obtain wealth, wives, and slaves was considered normal. They lived by the code of "eye for eye and tooth for tooth." Vengeance came upon anyone who dared to hurt or even insult them. Revenge was a way of life. Violence was quite normal for a people living in such a barbaric culture.[3]

Religion of Pre-Islamic Arabia
Mohammed Ibn Abdalla was born in this country in the city of Mecca in A.D. 570. The religion of the Arabs consisted in the worship of the sun, the moon, and the fixed stars. In their travels through nights in the desert, they familiarized themselves with the names, orders, and stations of the stars. Each tribe, each family, and each independent warrior chose the objects of his worship.[4] However, the holy place in Mecca, called the Caaba (Kabah) was the convergence of religious life.

Edward Gibbon described the Caaba and its religious importance as follows:

> The Caaba was a rectangular black stone chapel 72 feet long, 69 feet wide, and 81 feet high held in deep reverence by every Arabian. According to Mohammed, the Caaba was built by Abraham and his son, Ishmael. The last month of each year thousands of pilgrims presented their vows and offerings at this house of God. The same rites which are now accomplished by the faithful Muslim were invented and practiced by the superstition of the idolaters... Each tribe found or introduced in the Kabah their domestic worship: the temple was adorned or defiled with three hundred and sixty idols of men, eagles, lions, and antelopes.[5]

The Koreish or Quraysh tribe to which Mohammed belonged controlled the Kabah. This authority gave them much power politically, religiously as well as economically. In the Kabah was a small black stone about the size of a football that had been set up and adopted by this tribe. The custom was to kiss the stone, which was probably a meteorite. To this day, every Muslim pilgrim kisses the black stone during his pilgrimage to Mecca.[6]

Allah, the God of Quraysh Tribe
It is interesting to note that the Quraysh tribe into which Mohammed was born was particularly devoted to Allah. The name of Mohammed's father was Abd-Allah, and his uncle's name was Obied-Allah affirming their devotion to the god, Allah.[7] *The Concise Encyclopedia of Islam* helps clear up some confusion as to whether Allah and Jehovah are the same:

8

> ALLAH is the proper name of God among Muslims, corresponding in usage to Jehovah (Jahweh) among Hebrews. Thus it is not to be regarded as a common noun meaning 'God,' and the Muslim must use another word or form if he wishes to indicate any other than his own peculiar deity... he could never speak of Allah of the Christians or Allah of the Jews.... Muhammad found the Meccans believing in a supreme God whom they called Allah. With Allah, however, they associated other minor deities, some evidently tribal, others called daughters of Allah... Muhammad's reform was to assert the solitary existence of Allah.[8]

If the above statements are true, then Mohammed, as a result of his communications with the alleged Angel Gabriel, elevated Allah, the deity of the Quraysh tribe, to be the Creator of the universe. In so doing, he negated all the deities worshipped by the other Arabian tribes and established Allah as the only God and himself his prophet.

Arabia a Land of Refuge

Since Arabia was free, it was a refuge for persecuted sects seeking asylum and safety. Seven hundred years before the death of Mohammed, Jews migrated to Arabia. After the fall of Jerusalem under the persecution of Hadrian and Titus, Roman generals, there was a greater influx of Jews. Christian communities were present. Both Jews and Christians formed a formidable community in Arabia. Sadly, the Christianity that took root in Arabia was heretical, such as the Marcionites and the Manicheans, with their apocryphal gospels and defective doctrines of Christ and the trinity.[9] The Jews and Christians were known as the people of the Book. According to Bruce Metzer in *Early Versions of the Bible,* the actual date of the first translation into Arabic is not known. It was sometimes between 900—1200.[10] Gibbon has this to say about the influence of the Bible on the Arabs:

> In the story of Hebrew patriarchs the Arabs were pleased to discover the fathers of their nation. They applauded the birth and promises of Ishmael; revered the faith and virtue of Abraham;

traced his pedigree and their own to the creation
of the first man, and imbibed with equal credu-
lity the prodigies of the holy text, and the dreams
and the traditions of the Jewish rabbis.[11]

In our study the time has come to look at one of the most
remarkable men in the history of the world, Mohammed Ibn
Abdalla.

End Notes:

1. Gibbon, Edward, *The Decline and Fall of the Roman Empire,* Harcourt Brace and Company, New York, pp. 649, 650, 652.
2. Ibid., pp. 658, 653, 655.
3. Ibid., p. 656.
4. Ibid., pp. 658, 659.
5. Ibid., 659, 660.
6. Trifvocic, Serge, *The Sword of the Prophet—Islam history, theology, impact on the world,* Regina Orthodox Press, Boson, MA, 2002, p. 21.
7. Encyclopedia Britannica, p. Vol. A, p. 35.
8. Glasse', Cyril, *The Concise Encyclopedia of Islam,* Harper and Row Publishers, Inc., San Francisco, No date, p. 326.
9. Gibbon, pp. 660, 661
10. Metzer, Bruce, *Early Versions of the Bible,* Oxford Press, London, p. 260-268.
11. Gibbon, p. 662.

Over one billion people worldwide revere this man as the Apostle of Allah and believe that to him the Angel Gabriel revealed the Koran, which to Muslims is the divine word of Allah. At the same time, there are over two billion people worldwide who profess to believe that Jesus of Nazareth is the incarnate Son of God and the Holy Bible the inspired word of God. A proverb says, "the beauty is in the eye of the beholder." Those who believe Mohammed is the Apostle of Allah cannot and will not admit any defect in him. For a Muslim to even entertain such an idea would place him in mortal danger. The Tribune News Service July 14, 2003 gives this report:

> A professor in Iran allegedly insulted Islam, and his punishment is death, a ten-year ban from teaching, and eight-year exile, and 74 lashes. Pundits are not sure in what order the punishments will come.[1]

Those of us who are not Muslims are free to stand back and study the words and actions of this man, Mohammed. We have the inalienable right to discover for ourselves whether his truth claims are valid or not. His early followers wrote copiously of his sayings and activities. His famed biographers relate details of his life that cause consternation among Muslims when these facts are brought to light. In this study, the author makes no accusations against Mohammed or Islam, but he will freely look into the life of Mohammed as revealed in the Koran and the Hadith (Sacred writings containing anything Mohammed said, did, or gave silent approval). We also will note what historians have to say about him. The aim is to tell the truth.

Mohammed's Parents

Abdullah, was born into the Hashim clan of the Quraysh tribe and married a young woman named Aminah. After being married only six months, he joined a caravan heading for Syria and Damascus. This young husband never got to see his son, Mohammed, as he died on the return trip. The tearful mother gave her son a strange name, Mohammed, which had never been used among the Arabs. The name means "highly praised."

When Mohammed was five years old, his mother decided to visit her relatives in Medina and to visit her husband's grave. On the return trip, she also died. Mohammed was sent to live with his grandfather, Abdel Muttalib. A couple of years later he died and Mohammed went to live with this man's son. By the age of ten, Mohammed had been orphaned three times.[2]

Mohammed was well respected by his peers, and by his early twenties, had developed a reputation for honesty and integrity. A rich widow hired Mohammed to lead her caravans. Khadijah, forty years of age, fell in love and married her young employee, Mohammed, who was twenty-five years old. They had four daughters and two sons. Both sons died in infancy. The couple lived in a monogamous relationship for twenty-five years.[3]

Description of Mohammed

Edward Gibbon in the *Decline and Fall of The Roman Empire* enlightens us concerning Mohammed's appearance and conduct.

> According to the tradition of his companions, Mohammed was distinguished by the beauty of his person... They applauded his commanding presence, his piercing eye, his gracious smile, his flowing beard, his gestures that enforced each expression of the tongue... His memory was capacious and retentive, his wit easy and social, his imagination sublime, his judgment clear and decisive.[4]

Mohammed's Call

Hating the idolatry, degeneracy, and commercialization of religion in his hometown, Mohammed often resorted to the hills and caves outside Mecca to fast and meditate.[5] As a result of these times of isolation, Mohammed began to receive visitations and revelations. At first, Mohammed was frightened by these experiences. He was doubtful of the source of these revelations and expressed these fears to his wife. An account of his expressions of fear that the visitations were demonic and his wife's assurance that they were from Allah can be read in many accounts of Mohammed's biographies.[6]

To even consider that Mohammed could have been an epileptic or demon possessed naturally causes Muslims great consternation. But they must be reminded that these are not stories concocted by the enemies of Islam but these are possibilities recorded in their own holy books.

In McClintock and *Strong's Encyclopedia* we read the following:

> Muhammad was endowed with a nervous constitution and a lively imagination. It was not at all unnatural for him to come after a time to regard himself as actually called of God to build up his people in a new faith.
>
> Muhammad, as we gather from the oldest and most trustworthy narratives, was epileptic, and as such, was considered to be possessed of evil spirits.
>
> At first, he believed the saying, but gradually came to the conclusion, confirmed by his friends, that demons had no power over so pure and pious a man as he was, and he conceived the idea that he was not controlled by evil spirits, but that he was visited by angels whom he, disposed to hallucinations, a vision, an audition, afflicted with the morbid state of body and mind, saw in dreams... what seemed to him good and true after such epileptic attacks, he esteemed revelation in which he, at least in the first stages of his pathetic course, firmly believed and which imparted to his pensive, variable character, the necessary courage and endurance to brave all mortification and perils.[7]

Just as Muslims have the right to interpret the claims of Mohammed as divine revelations, the non-Muslim has the right to come to his own conclusions based on historical evidence.

After the first revelation, there was a silence of three years. During a time of great discouragement even his faithful wife asked, "Does it not seem that your Lord is displeased with you?" Mohammed sought refuge at Mt. Hira. Suicidal thoughts plagued him until he finally got peace that his call was from Allah.[8]

Mohammed Begins Ministry in Mecca

Mohammed began to preach his message in Mecca. He confided to his wife Khadijah, "But whom shall I call and who will listen?" After a few moments of reflection, she replied, " I will be the first to listen." Thus, a woman became the first convert to Islam.[9]

At the first, Mohammed was content to use the argument of persuasion in his attempt to convert his tribesmen, the Jews, and the Christians. The Meccans resented his attack upon their idols, their drunkenness, their fornications and considered him a threat to their financial welfare. Angry Meccans began to harass any Muslim who came near the Kabah to pray. Some of the poets would follow Mohammed around and shout "Madman! Madman!" They wrote slanderous poems and quoted them in the market place. After 13 years of severe struggle and danger, Mohammed and his converts fled to Medina. The Meccans, the Jews, and the Christians rejected the new prophet and his message.[10] In Mecca, Mohammed was the Rasul (Messenger) of Allah. An honest observation would be that Mohammed failed as a preacher.

The Hejira

A group of people from Yathrib (Medina) while visiting Mecca accepted Mohammed's message and invited him to come to their city. On his arrival in A.D. 622, the whole city welcomed him as a hero. The Hejira or flight to Medina was such a momentous event that the Muslim calendar begins from that date.[11] In Medina, Mohammed changed his tactics. He immediately became the city's religious, political, and military leader. From then on Mohammed would be the Generalissimo of Allah. In this role, he was eminently successful. By raiding and looting rich caravans, his religion became more attractive to the Arabs, and whole tribes began to say the Shahadah (confession), i.e., "There is no god but Allah and Mohammed is His Prophet" and to join his army.[12]

Battle for Arabia

The Meccans, realizing the rising strength of the Muslims, sent a large force and engaged in what is called the battle of Uhud. Mohammed lost this battle, was struck in the mouth by a sword, lost several teeth, and almost died. Some of his followers defected because they had gone into battle expecting a great victory, and it ended in defeat with their leader severely wounded. The Meccans failed to follow through to total victory.

After inflicting sufficient casualties to satisfy their lust for revenge, they returned to their towns and villages.[13]

There were many battles between the Muslims and the Meccans, but the battle of the Ditch was the largest and most crucial. In an effort to end Mohammed's threat once and for all, the Meccans became allies with numerous tribes throughout Arabia and approached Medina with an army of 10,000, the largest army ever assembled in Arabia. The Muslims dug a large deep ditch all along the exposed front section of the city of Medina, while the walls in the rear of the city could be blocked and fortified. For almost a month, the frustrated Meccans tried to breach the ditch, but their men were beaten back by a rain of arrows. Dissension in the ranks of the Meccan coalition, which was followed by a sandstorm caused the alliance to fall apart. The once proud coalition dissolved, and they quit the siege.[14]

Capture of Mecca

The Muslim victory over the Meccans and their allies elevated their status among the tribes of Arabia. Numerous tribal chiefs were converting, and it seemed that the Muslims could soon mount an attack and defeat their enemies. However, during the annual pilgrimage to Mecca and the Kabah, fourteen hundred unarmed Muslim pilgrims were sent from Medina. As a result, the stunned idolaters sent representatives to Mohammed in Medina to work out a ten-year peace treaty. The treaty was short lived as a tribe friendly to Mecca attacked a caravan of Muslims. Mohammed retaliated by leading an army of 10,000 to Mecca, and the city quickly surrendered to him.[15]

A modern Islamic historian or revisionist relates the conquest in this manner:

> The Meccans surrendered peacefully that night, and the next morning Mohammed led the victorious Muslims in a triumphal march into the city. When his soldiers took up positions throughout the city, he led a column toward the Kabah and found a large throng of Meccans standing there. These were the people who had tortured him and his followers for years. They called out to him, "What are you going to do with us?" He replied, "You are all forgiven today. Go back to your homes. You are all free."[16]

Mohammed's Revenge

However, according to the record of ancient Muslim historians, that is not what happened. An Arab poetess named Asma bint Marwan wrote couplets shaming the men of Medina for flocking to this stranger from Mecca. When her poem was read to Mohammed, he took action.

> On hearing these lines Muhummad said, "Will no one rid me of this daughter of Marwan?" One zealous Muslim, Umayr Adi, decided to execute the Prophet's wishes, and that very night crept into the writer's home while she lay sleeping, surrounded by her young children. There was even one at her breast. Umayr removed the suckling babe and then plunged his sword into the poetess. "Next morning, in the mosque at prayer, Mahomet [Muhammad]. Who was aware of the bloody design, said to Omeir [Umayr]: 'Hast thou slain the daughter of Marwan?' 'Yes, he answered; 'but tell me now, is there cause for apprehension?' 'None', said Mahomet; 'a couple of goats will hardly knock their heads together for it.' " Muhammad then praised him in front of the Muslims gathered in the mosque for his services to God and his Prophet.[17]

It must be emphasized that eminent ancient Muslim historians penned these accounts. These are only a sampling of such petty murders done at the behest of Mohammed. Many more could be related, but enough has been said. These were, after all, infidels who opposed Allah and his holy prophet. It was Allah's will that they be put to death.

Mystery of Kissing the Black Stone

After the surrender of Mecca to Mohammed and his forces, the first act was to cleanse the Kabah. All the gods, godesses, and fetishes were removed except one. The Black Stone that was worshipped by the Quraysh tribe was allowed to remain. Mohammed did not abolish the stone but kissed it as had been done before when the people worshipped this stone. Not only did he kiss it but ordered his followers to kiss it much to their surprise and objection. In his Sahih (part 2, page 183), al-Bukhari records a famous statement made by 'Umar ibn Khattab, which demonstrates the confusion of the Muslims. Bukhari says as follows:

> When 'Umar ibn al-Khattab reached the Black Stone, he kissed it and said, 'I know that you are a stone that does not hurt or benefit. If I had not seen the prophet kiss you, I would not have kissed you.[18]

All scholars (ancient and modern) confirm that this quote is authentic. It is well known that Muslim pilgrims jostle around to kiss it, as Mohammed and his companions did before them. Because of such crowding, the pilgrims suffer a large number of serious casualties. On a recent trip to the Orient I read this article form *The Independent*, a newspaper in Dhaka, Bangladesh, February 5, 2004, AP, Mina, Saudi Arabia.

> 8 Bangladeshis among 244 Killed in Mina Stampede. At least 244 people including eight Bangladeshis were trampled to death and hundreds more were hurt on February 4 under the crush of worshippers in one of the deadliest disasters during the annual Muslim pilgrimage to Saudi Arabia. The stampede occurred during the stoning of the devil, an emotional Haji ritual. Pilgrims frantically throw rocks, shout insults or hurl their shoes at three stone pillars—acts that are supposed to demonstrate their deep disdain for Satan. "Safety measures were in place at the site—one where fatal stampedes have been frequent—but caution isn't stronger than fate," said Saudi Haji Minister Iyad Madari. "All precautions were taken to prevent such an incident, but this is God's will." Similar incidents happened in 1998, 2001 and last year.

Verse of the Sword

Arabia had been captured by Islam. Still there were those who resisted and others who had professed to become Muslims but who were apostatizing. It was in this context that Surah 9:5

which has come to be known as the verse of the sword was revealed to Mohammed:

> So when the sacred months have passed away, then slay the idolaters wherever you find them, and take them captives and besiege them and lie in wait for them in every ambush, then if they repent and keep up prayer and pay the poor-rate, leave their way free to them; surely Allah is Forgiving, Merciful.

The *Jalalan* is a commentary which was published in 1983 by the Azhar University located in Cairo, Egypt (page 153), clarifies the message of Surah 9:5 like this:

> The Chapter of Repentance was revealed to raise the level of security which the infidels enjoyed because Mohammed had earlier made a covenant with them not to kill them. After that, this verse was given (9:5) in order to free God and Mohammed from any covenant with the infidels. It gives them four months in which they will be protected, but by the end of the four months (the end of the grace period), the order comes: Kill the infidels wherever you find them. Capture them, besiege them in their castles and fortresses until they are forced to accept Islam or be killed.[19]

After the conquest of Arabia for Islam, Mohammed wrote letters to neighboring countries inviting them to accept Allah and him as his prophet. But Mohammed died shortly after the conquest of Arabia, and it was left to his companions to break out of Arabia and go forth to conquer North Africa and Spain.[20] At one time, it looked as if Islam would conquer the world, but Charles Martel of France defeated the Muslims at the battle of Tours in 732 and their advance was stopped.

Mohammed and His Wives

It is common knowledge that Mohammed had many wives. This is a sore spot for many Islamic apologists. Yahiya Emerick's *The Complete Idiot's Guide to Understanding Islam* attempts to set the issue straight.

> Some Western scholars have charged that Muhammad was licentious on account of the many marriages he contracted. Popular myth has maligned the Prophet and cast a shadow over an otherwise universally accepted great leader. But what was the nature of these marriages, and do they demonstrate a weakness for pleasure? Let's examine the issue more closely... After the death of his first wife, Khadijah, he remarried only at the insistence of his companions, and his new wife was an overweight widow. His next marriage was to the daughter of his friend Abu Bakr. Contrary to what is commonly assumed, this girl named, A'isha, was not nine years old when the marriage took place. When the engagement was announced she was twelve and the actual marriage did not take place until she was sixteen. All the rest of Muhammad's marriages occurred in Medina and were spread over 10 years... Muhammad divided his time with each equally and helped with the housework in each wife's apartment. Again, if he were addicted to sex, he would have married all young women. Instead, they were mostly old and/or widowed.[21]

In our modern jargon this is called "spin." The documentation for all the women in Mohammed's harem is so vast and has been presented so many times by able scholars that only those who use circular reasoning or "spin" can deny it. Ali Dashti, Muslim scholar and statesmen, gives a list of the women in Mohammed's life. According to him there were 22 women in his harem. The first 16 were wives, numbers 17 and 18 were slaves or concubines, and the last four were neither wives nor concubines who freely chose to live with him.[22]

Women's Rights in the Koran

The Koran gives this advice to husbands concerning their wives.

> Men are the maintainers of women because Allah has made some of them to excel others and because they spend out of their property; the

good women are therefore obedient, guarding the
unseen as Allah has guarded; and (as to) those
on whose part you fear desertion, admonish
them, and leave them alone in the sleeping-
places and beat them; then if they obey you, do
not seek a way against them; surely Allah is High,
Great. Surah 4:34.

Allah to the Rescue

Mohammed's marriages can be separated into three catego-
ries: amorous, diplomatic, and tribal relationships. His first
marriage to Khadijah was clearly one of mutual devotion, love
and duty. The most famous of these tribal marriages was his
eighth wife, Zaynab. Zaynab married Zaid, Mohammed's
adopted son. Mohammed married his adopted son's wife but
was troubled by the proposition of marrying his daughter-in-
law.[23] This dilemma was solved by a revelation from Allah.

Surah 33:37 says, And when you said to him to
whom Allah had shown favor and to whom you
had shown a favor: Keep your wife to yourself
and be careful of (your duty to) Allah; and you
concealed in your soul what Allah would bring
to light, and you feared men, and Allah had a
greater right that you should fear Him. But when
Zaid had accomplished his want of her, We gave
her to you as a wife, so that there should be no
difficulty for the believers in respect of the wives
of their adopted sons, when they have accomplished their want of them; and Allah's command
shall be performed.

No comment!

Mohammed's Death

Mohammed conducted one final pilgrimage to Mecca when
he was nearing 63 years of age. He delivered a famous address
known as his Farewell Speech. Then he returned to Medina
where he continued to grow weaker. After suffering several days
of intense fever, Mohammed is said to have raised his eyes to
Heaven and called out, "Better the next world on high." With
his head resting in his beloved A'isha's lap, Mohammed passed
away.[24] Thus ended the life of one of the most influential and
controversial men that ever lived.

Example to Follow

To answer the question whether Mohammed is an example to be followed, I am going to let three men answer it. One is a Christian who converted to Islam and the others are Muslim brothers, who converted to Christianity. First let us hear from Emerick, the Muslim convert.

> His (Mohammed's) life and mission touched upon the hearts of a people who were living in superstition and idolatry. The teachings he promoted uplifted the status of women, gave rights to the poor, regulated the moral and social life of his followers, and provided a path to salvation for millions. Michael Hart, in his book, *The One Hundred Most Influential People,* ranked Muhammad as the most important person who ever affected our world because of his example, success, and enduring message. He was able to successfully fuse the tenets of religion and politics on a level no one has been able to do since. Writers from Washington Irvin to Mahatma Gandhi have praised him for his sincerity and noble character. Such was Muhammad, the Messenger of Allah: 'Philosopher, orator, apostle, legislator, warrior, conqueror of ideas, restorer of rational dogmas, of a cult without images; the founder of twenty terrestrial empires and of one spiritual empire, that is Muhammad. As regards all standards by which human greatness may be measured, we may well ask, is there a man greater than he?[25]

Ergen and Emir Caner are brothers of Turkish descent and were raised as Sunni Muslims by their father who was a leader of the Mosque. Both men are professors in Christian seminaries. To answer the question is Mohammed an example to follow this is their answer.

> Is Muhammad someone to be followed as the perfect example of obedience to God? The answer must be a resounding no. How can we trust his revelations and visions when he expressed doubt that they were revelations and sometimes thought himself to be demon-possessed? Muhammad's own foster mother, Halima, admit-

ted that she thought he was 'possessed by the devil.'

Also, how can we believe revelations from God when Muhammad himself either changed or modified them? His carelessness with the very words of Allah, words that he did not feel himself obliged to follow, casts a shadow on his trustworthiness.

Morally, the actions of Muhammad sometimes seem reprehensible. He killed critics for speaking their minds, ordered the severe beating of a woman to retrieve information from her, had sexual relations with a child of nine. He was a ruthless general and raided caravans merely for financial gain to expand his movement. He even broke the rules of engagement when he fought during a sacred month. Nonetheless, he is praised as the most beloved prophet.

Any honest account of Muhammad's life can be summed up in the words complexity, expediency, and depravity. By any measure, the life on earth of Jesus Christ, the Son of God, far exceeds Muhammad's in integrity, grace, and wisdom.

Jesus never took another life. He did not demean women nor exploit young girls for social gain. Christ was the true picture of love. He came and was rejected, and while we were yet sinners, Christ died for us (Romans 5:8). Muhammad came to shed blood and slaughter those who disagreed with him. Christ came to seek and save those who were lost (Luke 19:1).

Muhammad unified a country, indeed much of the world, by focusing on a stone in Mecca. Jesus Christ unifies sinners under his own death and resurrection. No one questions the influence of both men, but the character of their influence is as different as the difference between peace and war.[26]

End Notes

1. *The Tribune News Service*, 7/14/03.
2. Emerick, p. 270.
3. Ibid.
4. Gibbon, p. 663.
5. Dashti, Ali, *Twenty Three Years: A Study of the Prophetic Career of Mohammed*, Mazda Publishers, Costa Mesa, CA, 1994, p. 14.
6. Ibid., p. 24.
7. McClintock and Strong, *Encyclopedia*, 6:406. See also Pfander, The Balance of Truth, pp. 343-348
8. Hykal, M.H., *Life of Muhammad*, American Trust Publications, Plainfield, IN, 1976, p. 79.
9. Emerick, p. 272.
10. Emerick, pp. 273, 276,
11. Ibid., p. 277.
12. Gabriel, Mark, *Islam and Terrorism—What the Quran really teaches about Christianity, violence and the goals of the Islamic jihad*, Charisma House, Lake Mary, Fl.,2001, p.72.
13. Emerick, p. 282.
14. Ibid., 283.
15. Ibid., p. 284.
16. Ibid.
17. Rodison, Maxime, *Muhammad*, Pantheon Books, New York, 1971, p. 174 and also quoted by Waraq,Ibn, *Why I am Not a Muslim*, Prometheus Books, Amherst, NY, 1995, p. 94.
18. Sha'ware, Sheik al, *Legal Opinions*, part 3, p. 176.
19. *Jalalan*, Al Azhar University Press, 1983, p. 153.
20. Emerick, p. 284.
21. Ibid., p. 285.
22. Dashti, pp. 123, 125.
23. Shorrosh. Anis, *Islam Revealed—A Christian Arab's View of Islam*, Thomas Nelson Publishers, Nashville, TN, 1988, pp. 62, 63.
24. Emerick, p. 286.
25. Ibid.
26. Caner, Ergun and Emir, *Unveiling Islam—An Insider's Look at Muslim Life and Beliefs*, Kregel Publications, Grand Rapids, MI, 2002, pp. 63, 64.

Americans are infamous for what they do not know about history. If the average American knows next to nothing about his own country's history, how much less does he know about Islamic history? Yet to get an intelligent grasp of the issues that are before us, familiarizing ourselves with the great movements of Islamic history is vital. Westerners have a hard time understanding why the Muslims do not like America and refer to our great benevolent nation as the Great Satan. Behind the animosity lies fourteen hundred years of political and religious struggle between Islam and Christianity.

The Caner brothers in *Unveiling Islam* point out seven momentous events in this struggle:

691	Dome of the Rock Mosque erected in Jerusalem
715	Great Mosque erected in Damascus
732	Battle of Tours in France checks Islam's advance across Europe
1095-1291	Crusades define bitter relations between Christianity and Islam for future centuries
1453	Ottoman Turks conquer the Byzantine Empire
1492	Roman Catholic Christianity enforced in Spain once more and Muslims driven out
1914—1918	Ottoman rulers make a fatal miscalculation in joining the Empire's fortunes with Kaiser Wilhelm[1]

Bernard Lewis, Professor Emeritus of Near Eastern Studies at Princeton University, has offered this overview of attacks and counterattacks, jihads and crusades, conquests and reconquests:

> For the first thousand years Islam was advancing, Christendom [was] in retreat and under threat. The new faith conquered the old Christian lands of the Levant and North Africa, and invaded Europe, ruling for a while in Sicily,

Spain, Portugal and even parts of France. For the past three hundred years, since the failure of the second Turkish siege of Vienna in 1683 and the rise of the European colonial empires in Asia and Africa, Islam has been on the defensive, and the Christian and post-Christian civilization of Europe and her daughters has brought the whole world, including Islam, within its orbit.[2]

Resurgence of Islam

The Caner brothers sum up the present situation so concisely that I want to quote them:

> Bernard Lewis's article, *The Roots of Muslim Rage,* appeared in *Atlantic Monthly* magazine in September 1990, exactly eleven years before the attacks on World Trade Centers and the Pentagon. During those years, Muslims fulfilled Lewis's expectation and returned in unprecedented numbers to their root proposition that the world lives in either the House of Islam or the House of Unbelief. From the Muslim standpoint, said Lewis, "The greater part of the world is still outside Islam, and even inside the Islamic lands, according to the views of the Muslim radicals, the faith of Islam has been undermined and the law of Islam has been abrogated. The obligation of holy war therefore begins at home and continues abroad, against the same infidel enemy.[3]

Financed by Petrodollars

Now that Islamic countries sit on top of rich oil reserves, this economic power gives them once again the ability to revert back to the strategy of attacking unbelievers of any race, creed, or background. This time it is not with frontal military assault but with the force of terrorism seeking to break the will of the West to resist. George Bush did not react the way they expected. The cold-hearted attacks on the World Trade Centers and the Pentagon united our country as never before, resulting in an all-out war against terrorism. American military power created havoc within the Taliban in Afghanistan and Suddam Hossain's regime in Iraq. The fact that all nineteen hijackers in the 9/11 attacks were from Saudi Arabia and surrounding Muslim Middle Eastern countries indicate that these Muslim countries or at least some of their citizens support terrorism.

Mohammed's Successor

Emerick speaks of the problems facing the Muslim community at the death of Mohammed:

> The Muslim community had to deal with a temporary crisis of faith after the death of the Prophet Mohammed. For 23 years he had guided his followers, teaching them a new tradition and acting as their spiritual and political leader. What would become of Islam without him? The Koran speaks of this matter in Surah 3:144 "And Muhammad is no more than an apostle; the apostles have already passed away before him; if then he dies or is killed will you turn back upon your heels? And whoever turns back upon his heels, he will by no means do harm to Allah in the least and Allah will reward the grateful.[4]

The Muslims continued in their faith, quickly elected a leader (Caliph or deputy successor) and put down several internal uprisings as well confronted dangerous external threats.

When Mohammed died in A.D. 632, Islam was for the first time without a leader. The Muslim community quickly met to discuss the choice of a new leader. The Medina converts desired one of their own to be the caliph, but Abu Bakr, a Meccan, was chosen because he was Mohammed's trusted friend and led the worship at the Mosque during Mohammed's final illness. In his acceptance speech he spoke conciliatory words to the Medina converts: "O people, I have been chosen to be your leader, even though I am no better than any of you. If I do right, help me. If I do wrong, correct me.[5]

Fate of Apostates

Abu Bakr picked up the sword and secured the Arabian Peninsula for Islam. It is noteworthy that after Mohammed died, most Arabians abandoned Islam and refused to pay their zakat (taxes) and do other Islamic duties. This rebellion led to what is called the Battles of Riddah or Apostasy.[6] Emerick, in his *The*

Idiot's Complete Guide to Islam defines apostasy like this: "Riddah means apostacy, renouncing your religion. It is a major crime in Islam and can result in capital punishment if the apostate turns into an enemy of the community."[7] Abu Bakr was obedient to Mohammed's command that there be no two religions in Arabia.[8] From that day till this day, all religious worship, symbols, or churches except Islam have been forbidden in the country of Arabia. Although his leadership was brief, only two years, his accomplishments for Islam were great.[9]

Umar ibn Khattab, Islam's Second Caliph

Abu Bakr handpicked Umar, and he was proclaimed caliph by acclamation. Umar was a brave soldier and a good administrator. Through his guidance Islam greatly extended its territory. At the beginning of his reign he defeated the Persians and took control of all the land west of the Euphrates River. The people welcomed him as a deliverer from Persian cruelties. At the same time in the West, the Muslim forces fighting the Byzantines (Christian Orthodox Church) were victorious in battle after battle. In most cases the cities were surrounded, supplies were cut off, and the cities surrendered without a battle. After the city of Damascus fell, the Byzantine Emperor in far away Turkey organized an army of 250,000 to fight the Muslims. In the year 637 at a place called Yarmuk, the Muslims won a decisive victory resulting in the capture of Palestine, Egypt, Syria, and Iraq.[10]

Umar organized the national Muslim government into eight provinces and appointed a governor over each. He also reorganized the system of tax collection and the treasury. After 10 years as caliph, Umar was stabbed by a Persian assassin. On his death bed, he appointed a committee to choose Uthman ibn Affan, "a trusted companion of the Prophet" as the next caliph.[11]

Trouble in the Camp

All was going well, and Muslims were making great strides on all fronts. Caliph Uthman ordered copies of the Koran to be placed in every major city. Gradually, reports of corruption on the part of Muslim governors reached Uthman. Some of these governors were so powerful they ignored the caliph's written orders. A group of people came to Medina to complain about the governors. A "fake" letter supposedly signed by Uthman was planted in the caravan ordering all the people who had come to complain to be killed when they returned home. The letter was found en route and the caravan returned to Medina. Uthman when confronted with the letter said the letter was a forgery. The mob refused to believe him and killed him in his own home.[12]

From that point things started to go down hill. Ali ibn Abi Taleb, Uthman's son-in-law and a cousin of Mohammed, became the third caliph. Aisha, Mohammed's widow, fought bitterly against Ali. A rebel group formed and slew those responsible for Uthman's death. The rival factions fought a famous battle called the battle of the Camel because Aisha rushed into the battle on a camel trying to stop the Muslims from fighting one another. Her camel was killed, and she was escorted off the battlefield.[13]

Ali decided to remove all the corrupt governors that were appointed by Uthman. However, the governor of Syria, Mu'awiya, refused to step down and came to fight Ali with an army. Ali and Mu'awiya tried to find a compromise, which resulted in Ali's men turning against him. In 661, Ali was assassinated. Another assassin assigned to kill Mu'awiya failed in his attempt. Under Mu'awiya's undisputed leadership the head of government moved to Damascus and became a monarchy.[14]

Successful Jihad

After Ali's death, the internal turmoil ceased and Islam set its goal to conquer the world. Consider how successful was their jihad (holy war). From A.D. 622, which is the date of the Hejira (flight to Medina), through 732, Muslims were making such progress it looked as if they would conquer the world for Allah and Mohammed his prophet. All of Arabia came under Islamic rule by 632. Cypress fell in 647, Tunisia, Kabul, Afghanistan and Constantinople in 670, North Africa in 700, Spain in 711, the Chinese Turkestan border in 715, and Morocco in 722. Muslim rule stretched from the border of China to the border of France.[15]

Tide Turns

The seemingly unstoppable expansion halted at the border of France at the battle of Tours. The importance of the outcome of this battle cannot be overestimated. If France had fallen, then Italy, the center of Western Christianity, would have been an easy prey. Charles Martel and his brave soldiers saved Europe from Islam. Paul Halsal on his website, in the article Medieval Sourcebook: Arabs, Franks, and the Battle of Tours, 732 described the battle like this:

> For almost seven days the two armies watched one another, waiting anxiously the moment for joining the struggle. Finally they made ready for combat. And in the shock of the battle the men of the North....stood, one close to another, form- ing as it were a bulwark of ice; and with great blows of their swords they hewed down the Ar- abs. Drawn up in a band around their chief, the people of the Austrasians carried all before them. Their tireless hands drove their swords down to the breasts [of the foe].[16]

Praise God for Charles Martel and his brave soldiers. Without a doubt the hand of God orchestrated the outcome of this battle.

End Notes

1. Caner, p. 67.
2. Lewis, Bernard, *"The Roots of Islam's Rage,"* Atlantic Monthly, September, 1990, pp. 47-60.
3. Caner, p. 68.
4. Emerick, p. 287.
5. Emerick, p. 289 quoting Rafi Ahmed Fidai, *Concise History of Muslim World,* p. 68.
6. Ibid.
7. Ibid.
8. Gabriel, Mark, *Islam and the Jews—The Unfinished Battle,* Charisma House, Lake Mary, FL., 2003, p. 114.
9. Ibid.
10. Ibid. pp. 290, 291.
11. Ibid., p. 292.
12. Ibid., pp. 293,294.
13. Ibid., p. 292, 293-295.
14. Ibid, pp. 294, 295.
15. Caner, p. 71.
16. Halsal, Paul, on his website, www.Medieval Sourcebook: *Arabs, Franks, and the Battle of Tours,* 732.

From A.D. 750—1258 Islamic culture zenithed. After much in-fighting and bloodletting, the Abbasids removed the Umayyads from power. Baghdad instead of Damascus became the new capital.[1] The time was ripe for progress. With no exterior military threat, unlimited slave labor, and riches gathered from around the world—coupled with a confluence of Indian, Persian and Greek culture—Baghdad rose to great prominence. "The city of Baghdad, known as the jewel of the world, was founded as a unique fortress city built in the shape of a wheel with all roads leading to the palace in the center."[2]

Islamic Utopia

While Europe endured the Dark Ages under despotic popes, the Middle East was flourishing with intellectual light. The Muslim writer, Yahiya Emerick is given to exaggeration and spin, but his remarks concerning Islam's golden age are interesting:

> In fact, for most of the last thousand years it was the Muslim world that was advancing on all fronts and the Christian world that was lagging behind in the arts and sciences. During the Abbasid caliphate, Muslim cities were the largest in the world, with well-established social services and a cultural vibrancy that caused Europeans to marvel. Free public hospitals, universities, local public health inspectors, even paved roads were every day parts of life for citizens in Muslim lands.
>
> The Islamic world was a cosmopolitan mix of people of all races and colors who spoke dozens of different languages (Arabic was the *lingua franca,* being the religiously sanctioned tongue). The mighty caravan routes were much like superhighways are today and were filled with traffic and congestion. International business was booming, and merchants could rely on writing checks that would be honored at banks throughout the Muslim world. Travel was easier than at

any time in human history, and the practice of medicine was no longer a quack's profession, with aspiring doctors required to pass exams. The Islamic world, in short, was much like modern America with the exception of the technology available today.[3]

Mongol Conquest

As with all things human, decadence set in. The Caliphs became more and more sensual and corrupt. Local warlords and charismatic leaders carved several semi-independent states out of the empire. The whole glorious Aabbasid Empire crashed in 1258 as the Mongol hordes swept into Muslim lands like a tidal wave. A Muslim historian describes the unbelievable events:

> They conquered all of Muslim Persia and Iraq and unleashed a reign of terror against the populace eclipsed only by Adolph Hitler's Nazi war machine. It is estimated that over 16 million people were massacred in Persia and Iraq alone. (It took the Mongols 40 days to execute the entire population of Baghdad.) Libraries were burnt, cities were razed, and the practice of Islam was forbidden under Mongol decree. Eventually, the Mongols converted to Islam. Later Mongol rulers restored mosques, reopened schools, and adopted the cultures of the lands they lived in. They went on to conquer nearly all of Hindu India, and a large part of southern Russia and eastern Europe for Islam.[4]

Crusades

No other event has defined Muslim-Christians relations to such a degree as the Crusades. From 1095—1270 Christian armies invaded the Holy Land seeking to reclaim the holy places from the Muslims. Islamist apologists take a different view blaming the Christians as aggressors and the Muslims as victims. Serge Trifkovic in his book, *The Sword of the Prophet—Islam History, Theology, Impact on the World,* gives a historical perspective to the Crusades as follows:

> The Crusades were but a temporary setback to Islamic expansion, and the source of endless ar-

guments that sought to establish some moral equivalence between Muslims and Christians at first, and eventually to elevate the former to victimhood and condemn the latter as aggressors. Far from being wars of aggression, the Crusades were a belated military response of Christian Europe to over three centuries of Muslim aggression against Christian lands, the systemic mistreatment of the indigenous Christian population of those lands, and harassment of Christian pilgrims. The post-modern myth, promoted by Islamic propagandists and supported by some self-hating Westerners—notably in the academy—claims that the peaceful Muslims, native to the Holy Land, were forced to take up arms in defense against European-Christian aggression. This myth takes A.D. 1095 as its starting point, but it ignores the preceding centuries, starting with the early caliphs, when Muslim armies swept through the Byzantine Empire, conquering about two-thirds of the Christian world of that time.[5]

UnChristian Jihad

The Crusades originated as a joint venture of Pope Urban II and Emperor Alexius of the Byzantine Empire uniting to resist the Turks invasion seeking control of Christian lands. Peter the Hermit successfully motivated the armies against what he called the "Evil Empire of Mahound (Mohammed)."[6] Serge Trifkovic describes this sad unChristian capture of Jerusalem like this:

> It was not until April 1099 that the Crusader army marched on to Jerusalem, and on June 7 besieged the city. The attack began July 14, 1099—the date destined to live in antiChristian infamy centuries later—and the next day the Crusaders entered Jerusalem from all sides and slew its inhabitants, regardless of age or sex. The soldiers of the Church Militant, as it turned out, could not only outfight but also out-massacre their Mohammedan foes.[7]

Without a doubt the debacle of the Crusades inflicted great damage on the cause of Christ. What the Crusaders did to the Muslim inhabitants of Jerusalem in 1099 was as bad as what the Muslims had done to countless Christian cities before and after this time. However, the carnage was less pardonable because unlike the Muslims, it was not justifiable by Christian tenets. All of this contradicts the teachings of Christ. He told Peter *"Put up again thy sword into his place: for all they that take the sword shall perish with the sword"* (Matthew 26:52). The Apostle Paul told us, *"For the weapons of our warfare are not carnal, but mighty through God to the pulling down of strongholds"* (II Corinthians 10:4). Instead of slaughtering our enemies, we are commanded to love them. Jesus said concerning our enemies, *"But I say unto you, Love your enemies, bless them that curse you, do good to them that hate you, and pray for them which despitefully use you and persecute you"* (Matthew 5:44). God, of course, was not in this travesty called the Crusades. Evil men masquerading as the servants of Christ through the Crusades did irreparable damage to the cause of Christ and His true Church.

Ottoman Empire

After the Mongol invasion devastated Baghdad and surrounding areas, the Ottoman Empire had its beginning with a band of frontier warriors from Turkey. Gradually they became more powerful and built what was the greatest of the Muslim empires. The famous Tamerlane was an Ottoman Turk. "In 1453 the Ottomans seized Constantinople, bringing to an end the eleven-hundred-year tenure of the Byzantine Empire and establishing themselves as successors to the Roman Empire."[8]

Mehmed, the conqueror of Constantinople, saw himself as successor to both Roman Emperors and Arab Caliphs. The Ottoman Turks had grand ideas of world domination combined with Islamic jihad. For over two centuries, the Ottomans were a definite threat to Europe. In 1529 they laid siege to Vienna and once again in 1683.[9] The European armies made use of mercenaries, professional soldiers. The Turks had a slave army. They had a systematic recruitment of slaves [Christian boys] whom they converted to Islam, trained in elite schools to become military officers and government servants.[10] "The non-Muslims were considered *dhimmis* or protected people, subject to a special tax and some discriminatory measures."[11]

The cruelty of the Ottoman Turks must be told. Very few Americans have ever heard of the genocide in Armenia. In the awful annals of the twentieth century, two instances of genocide stand out. The Jewish holocaust of 1942-1945 has spawned a vast amount of literature, museums, and publicity. The other genocide, Armenia in 1877-1922, lies buried in a few history books. Armenia borders Turkey and was converted to the Christian religion in the year 301 in response to the missionary work of one Gregory the Illuminator.[12] Let us hear from one whose family severely suffered in this genocide:

> "My mother was born in 1902. When she was eight or ten years old, there was in the Near East a holocaust, genocide, before those terms had come into our language.
>
> The Muslim Turks set out to destroy the Armenian Christian population, which was under their power in Eastern Turkey. They were ordered to go through the villages and kill all the men. That would guarantee within a generation or two the virtual decimation of the population. This was about 1912, just before World War I, and my mother was about ten years old. She remembers the Turkish soldiers coming into their village and into her home and killing her father in the presence of her mother, sister and young brother. My grandmother, my mother's mother, was very evidently pregnant; and one of the soldiers said to the other, "Let's rip her open and see if it is a boy." They did not. The other soldier replied, "Have you no fear of Allah?—that would have been going too far." They had just murdered my grandfather, but that would have been going too far. And they left. My mother was placed in an orphanage with her sister.[13]

How Could It Happen?

Robert Spencer in his book, *Islam Unveiled,* gives a horrifying example from history of what can happen where Muslims have the upperhand. Most Muslims are peace loving people seeking to live a normal life. However, in Islam, ordinary life can be disrupted by the call of religion. Radical Muslims have at times treated nonradical Muslims as one large sleeper cell that can be activated by a summons to the full practice of their religion. This is illustrated by a chilling story from the Ottoman Empire of the late nineteenth century:

> Then one night, my husband came home and told me that the padisha (Muslim religious leader) had sent word that we were to kill all the Christians in our village, and that we would have to kill our neighbors. I was very angry, and told him that I did not care who gave such orders, they were wrong. These neighbors had always been kind to us, and if he dared to kill them, Allah would pay us out. I tried all I could to stop him, but he killed them—killed them with his own hand.[14]

During World War I the Ottomans cast their lot with William Kaiser of Germany. This resulted in the demise of that empire. Having not learned their lesson, the Grand Mufti of Palestine and other Muslim nations cast their lot with Nazi Germany in World War II. There was a common bond that drew Hitler and the Muslim states together. It was the hatred of the Jew.[15]

Jihad Without End

From this short history lesson on Islam, it can truthfully be said that Islam from the beginning to the present, has been a religion of intolerance, a jihad without end. "William Muir, one of the greatest orientalists of all time (1819—1905), summed it up at the end of a long and distinguished career when he declared his convictions 'that the sword of Muhammad and the Qur'an are the most fatal enemies of civilization, liberty, and truth which the world has yet known.'[16] Look at the Muslim world today with Sudan, Iran, Saudi Arabia, Syria, the Taliban, etc., and it is easy to agree with the person who said "the Arab empire is an unmitigated cultural disaster parading as God's will, but parading, in its modern metamorphosis, as the creed of equality."[17]

The idea that Islam is a religion of tolerance, equality, and peace rules the day. It is a very popular mantra, the politically correct thing to say and believe. Anwar Shaikh seeks to set the record straight:

This fiction has been presented as a fact with an unparalleled skill. In fact, the Prophet Muhammad divided humanity into two sections, the Arabs and the non-Arabs. According to this categorization, the Arabs are the rulers, and the non-Arabs are to be ruled through the yoke of Arab cultural imperialism. Islam is the means to realize this dream, because its fundamentals raise superiority of Arabia sky-high, inflicting a corresponding inferiority on the national dignity of its non-Arab followers.... The Islamic love of mankind is a myth of even greater proportions. Hatred of non-Muslims is the pivot of Islamic existence. It not only declares all dissidents as the denizens of hell, but also seeks to ignite a permanent fire of tension between Muslims and non-Muslims; it is far more lethal than Karl Marx's idea of social conflict, which he hatched to keep his theory alive.[18]

End Notes:

1. Caner. p. 72.
2. Emerick, p.300.
3. Ibid. p. 301.
4. Ibid. p. 300.
5. Trifvocic, p. 97.
6. Ibid., p. 99.
7. Ibid.
8. Esposito, John, *The Oxford History of Islam,* Oxford University Press, New York, 1999, p. 374.
9. Lewis, p. 52.
10. Esposito., p. 386.
11. Ibid.
12. Panosian, Edward, *Islam and the Bible—Considering Islam Biblically,* Ambassador Emerald International, Greenville, SC, 2003, p. 2.
13. Ibid.
14. Pryce-Jones, David, *The Closed Circle, An Interpretation of the Arabs,* Ivan R. Dee, 2000, pp. 31,32.
15. Lewis, p. 59.
16. Trifvocic, p. 132.
17. Ibid.
18. Shaik, *Anwar, Islam: The Arab National Movement,* The Principality Publishers, U.K., 1995.

In this chapter, we are going to lay out in simple fashion the five pillars of Islam. Along the way we will define terms with which most Americans are not familiar. These five pillars are obligatory for every Muslim. They are non-negotiable, not to be questioned, but believed to the uttermost. To criticize the five pillars is tantamount to heresy or blasphemy punishable by death. All over the world, Muslims observe these five pillars, and it gives them a sense of unity and family.

The Creed — *Shahadah*

The first words a Muslim baby hears are "I declare there is no god but Allah, and I declare Mohammed is the Messenger of Allah." In his daily prayers a Muslim will repeat seventeen times the creed or *Shahadah*. The creed includes the two founding principles of Islam: There is only one God, and Mohammed is His prophet. The creed has a negation and an affirmation: no god but Allah and Mohammed is His prophet. The *Shahadah* is the defining statement of Islam. When a person desires to convert to Islam, all he or she need do is believe in what the *Shahadah* teaches and then recite it in front of witnesses. Voila! Another Muslim convert.

Daily Prayers — *Salat*

It is quite an impressive sight to see on a large field 10 or 20 thousand Muslim men going through their prayers kneeling, standing, bowing all in unison. Have you ever wondered what prayers they are praying? They are quoting verses from the Koran. Islam distinguishes between making personal requests to Allah (supplications) and ritual prayer for worship (Salat). The former is optional, but the ritual prayer is to be performed five times a day. The official prayer times are before sunrise, just after noon, late afternoon, just after sunset, and at night. Before prayer, Muslims wash their hands and feet and turn their faces toward Mecca. Islamic prayers are said in Arabic exclusively much the same way the Catholic priests pray in Latin.

Alms Giving — *Zakat*

The Zakat is to be given by every Muslim who has the means to do so. At least 2.5% of one's income is to be given to charitable purposes, to the Mosque, or some other religious work. This is welfare Islamic style. The rich pay more, and the poorer pay less. In Muslim countries, beggars line up at the gates of the rich, and part of a rich man's *zakat* is to feed the poor.

Fast — *Saum*

The fourth pillar of Islam is known as *Saum* or fasting. During the month of Ramadan, which is the ninth month in the Islamic calendar, Muslims are required to observe a strict fast from dawn till dusk. During the daylight hours, one must abstain from all foods, liquids, inhaled substances (cigarettes), and sexual activity. Some of the more devout do not swallow their saliva. During the nights of the month of the fast, Muslims feast as at no other time of the year. At the sighting of the moon at the end of the month of Ramadan, Muslims celebrate much like Christians do at Christmas by exchanging gifts, buying new clothes, feasting, and visiting friends. The celebration is called "Eid." In 2001, American Muslims petitioned the U.S. Postal Service to create a commemorative stamp for the Muslim fast of Ramadan. Naturally, the petition was granted.

Pilgrimage — *Hajj*

The fifth pillar of Islam is called the *Hajj*. Once a year two million Muslims from all over the world descend upon a desert oasis in Mecca, Saudi Arabia. The *Hajj* or pilgrimage occurs in the twelfth month of the Islamic calendar and continues for one week. The main feature is the Kabah or a cube shaped building made of brick and covered with black cloth. Muslims believe that Abraham and Ishmael built the Kabah. Inside the Kabah is a black stone about the size of a football, which every Muslim is to kiss because Mohammed kissed it. Running around the Kabah seven times and throwing stones at the Devil are a few of the activities of the pilgrims. Needless to say, this a highlight in the life of a Muslim. By the way, only Muslims are allowed to enter Mecca.

Holy War — *Jihad*

Although Jihad is not one of the five pillars of Islam, it sums up the essence of Islam. Muslims talk about the "greater" Jihad and the "lesser" Jihad. The greater Jihad is a struggle for personal piety or striving to overcome evil. The lesser Jihad is the defense of one's religion or territory. As has been pointed out in the history of Islam, Jihad is a continuous activity of conquering the world for Allah and Mohammed. Jihad is inherent in the Koran. Surah 2:193 reads. "And fight with them until there is no persecution, and religion should be only for Allah, but if they desist, then there should be no hostility except against the oppressors." "Persecution" means rejecting Islam. In his great book, *Secrets of the Koran*, Don Richardson points out how Muslim apologists twist the meaning of words to make Islam look docile.

> Amazingly, M.M. Ali (translator of the Koran into English) wants us to think that Mohammed in the above quote, actually advocates total freedom of religion! Ali writes: 'When persecution ceases and men are not forced to accept or renounce a religion, being at liberty to profess any religion of truth of which they are convinced, then there should be no more fighting.'
>
> Mr. Ali must know that Mohammed meant exactly the reverse: Fighting must continue until Islam is the only religion left in the Arabian Peninsula. Freedom of religion is one of the victims lying dead in the sands. Like many other apologists, Ali is little more than a spin doctor following Mohammed with whitewash and brush. He seeks to make even Mohammed's most bigoted statement sound tolerant.[1]

Anyone that has lived in a Muslim country knows that jihad is always on the mind of serious Muslims.

Now that we have explored the five pillars of Islam and a word about Jihad let us discuss what Muslims believe.

Belief in Allah

Their creed affirms belief in Allah. There is no god but Allah. Muslims believe that Allah is singular, i.e., without a partner. He is the Creator of the universe. They have given Allah ninety-nine names, such as Merciful, Magnificent, Mighty One, etc., but nowhere in the Koran does it call Allah "love." Allah does not reveal Himself; He reveals His will. Muslims believe it is Allah's will that all people submit to Him and to His prophet Mohammed. Those refusing to submit are considered enemies. In the Muslim mind, an enemy is not someone who is threatening harm to them but anyone who is not willing to submit to Allah, i.e., to become a Muslim.

Belief in Angels

Gabriel, an angel, plays an important role in Islam. He is the angel that dictated the Koran to Mohammed. Muslims believe in good angels and bad angels. The bad angels are called jinn. Muslims believe that an angel resides on each shoulder. The one on the right records good deeds; the one on the left evil deeds.

Belief in Four Holy Books

Muslims believe in four divine revelations: Torah given to Moses; Jabur given to David; Injil (Good News) given to Jesus; and Koran given to Mohammed. At the beginning of his ministry while seeking to persuade the Christians and the Jews of his prophethood, he somewhat catered to them by calling them the "People of the Book" and having his disciples pray toward Jerusalem.[2] A study of the Koran reveals multiple discrepancies between the Bible and the Koran. For example, surah 4:157, "We killed Christ Jesus the son of Mary, the Apostle of Allah, but they killed him not, nor crucified him, but so it was made to appear unto them." Again Surah 5:116 states that Christians worship three gods: the Father, the Mother (Mary), and the son (Jesus). A heretical sect of Christianity, the Cholodridians, believed this, and more than likely, Mohammed learned this heresy from them. Surahs 28:38 and 40:25 teach that Haman lived in Egypt during the time of Moses and built the tower of Babel. To get around these problems, Muslims say our Bible has been corrupted. Since this is such an important matter, it would be good to hear more about it from one who is very knowledgeable, Mark Gabriel, one time professor at Al Azha University in Cairo, Egypt.

> The corruption of Scripture raises a lot of questions. Where are the original uncorrupted copies? Muslims say, "They disappeared." They have nothing to show what the original books said. They cannot say when the corruption happened—just that it was long before the days of Muhammad. They can't say who did it or what was changed. There is no proof at all.

Muslim scholars theorize that Christians took out the parts of the New Testament that prophesied Muhammad would come. They say that Christians added parts about the trinity, Jesus being God's son, Jesus dying on the cross and salvation by the blood of Jesus.[3]

They also believe in abrogation. A later teaching in the Koran can abrogate an earlier teaching. For example, prayers were to be directed toward Mecca abrogating a previous command which said they were to be directed toward Jerusalem. Muslims believe that Mohammed was the seal of the prophets and he has the last true word from Allah.

Belief in Prophets

Islam has great respect for prophets. Muslims believe that Allah has sent 124,000 of them. Only twenty-five are mentioned in the Koran. The chief ones are Adam, Noah, Abraham, David, John the Baptist (Yahiya), Jesus, and Mohammed. Muslims believe that all the prophets were Muslims, i.e., submitted to Allah of Islam. Mohammed, of course, is the seal or the last of the prophets and by far the greatest.

Belief in Predestination

Allah wills all things good and bad. Muslims believe your fate is written on your forehead. This makes them very fatalistic. There is no freedom of the will in Islam. En sh'alla means "Allah wills it." One of the foundational teachings of Islam is the absolute sovereignty of Allah to the point of determinism. Allah knows everything, determines everything, decrees everything, and orders everything. Note this sentence from the Koran that teaches Allah is the cause of evil:

> Surah 17:16 says, "And when We wish to destroy a town, We send Our commandment to the people of it who lead easy lives, but they transgress therein; thus the word proves true against it, so We destroy it with utter destruction."

Allah orders the people who are prosperous to transgress. They follow His orders to transgress. As a result, He destroys them.

Belief in Judgment

Islam lays much emphasis upon the Judgment Day. On this day the good and evil deeds of Muslims will be put on a scale. Those Muslims having sufficient personal merit combined with the mercy of Allah will go to heaven. The joys and glories of paradise are tangible and sensual. Buy a Koran and read all about the houris or beautiful virgins, the intoxicating wines, etc., i.e., in Surah 44:54 which says, "Thus (shall it be), and We will wed them with Houris pure, beautiful ones." The Muslims that do not make the grade will suffer the fires of hell until their sins are purged. The belief is very similar to the Catholic's purgatory. What about the Jews, Christians, pagans, secularists, humanists, atheists, agnostics, etc.? The Koran graphically describes the torments that await all unbelievers: hellfire, brimstone, and much more!

This is just a cursory glance for beginners of Islamic practices and beliefs. The Islamic faith controls its adherents from the moment of birth to the moment of death. Definite guidelines are in place for every area of life. Without a doubt, Islam has much which is noble and good. Yet it stands as an intolerant faith, unwilling and unable, according to their holy book to live peacefully with those who refuse to say the shahadah.

From my perspective of studying Islam and living among Muslims for seventeen years, the distinctive between the Christian and the Islamic faith lies in the way we view our deity. The God of the Bible is holy, truthful, unchanging, and loving. As a result, He can never act in an unholy way or fail to keep His promise, change, or fail to love. His promises are sure and those who trust Him know that He will keep His promises.

Let me share a few Surahs from the Koran to show how Allah of the Koran and the God of the Bible are different.

First, Allah changes. Surah 2:106 says, "Whatever communications We abrogate (change) or cause to be forgotten, We bring one better than it or like it. Do you not know that Allah has power over all things? "

Second, Allah's concern for mankind is doubtful. Surah 32.13 says, "And if We had pleased We would certainly have given to every soul its guidance, but the word (which had gone forth) from Me was just: I will certainly fill hell with the jinn and men together."

Third, Allah deceives. Surah 8.30 says, "And when those who disbelieved devised plans against you that they might confine you or slay you or drive you away; and they devised plans and Allah too had arranged a plan; and Allah is the best of planners (deceivers)."

Fourth, Allah saves whom he will and punishes whom he

will. Surah 2.284 reads, "Whatever is in the heavens and whatever is in the earth is Allah's; and whether you manifest what is in your minds or hide it, Allah will call you to account according to it; then He will forgive whom He pleases and chastise whom He pleases, and Allah has power over all things."

The attributes of the God of the Bible and the Allah of the Koran are in no wise the same.

End Notes

1. Richardson, Don, *Secrets of the Koran,* Regal Books, Ventura, CA, 2003, p. 54.
2. Gabriel, *Islam and the Jews,* p. 71.
3. Ibid., p. 94.

INSUPERABLE DIFFERENCES
CHAPTER 7

Several years ago my son-in-law, a fellow preacher, and I had a meeting with the Imam of the Greenville mosque and a Roman Catholic turned Muslim. The thrust of their argument concerned the great similarities between Christianity and Islam. They proceeded to show us references to Islam and Mohammed in the Bible. Quoting the Koran they said, "Those who believe our revelations; those who follow the prophet who can neither read nor write, whom they will find described in the Torah and the Gospel (Surah 7:156-157). Of course, we proceeded to point out that there are great differences and to refute the false exegesis that they were using to find Islam and the Prophet Mohammed in the Bible. Their strategy for popularizing Islam included visiting churches to lecture on the similarities between the two faiths and to assure the churches that the two religions are almost the same.

Similarities between Islam and Christianity

Similarities there are. Both religions are monotheistic believing in one God who is the Creator of the universe. Both believe that Adam and Eve were the first human beings. Both believe in the existence and activities of angels. Prophets such as Noah, Abraham, David, and John the Baptist, are common to both. Both believe in a Day of Judgment. Both believe in a personal devil. Each claims to have a divine revelation from God. Each claims to have a special Revelator. The Koran says there is no god but Allah and Mohammed is His prophet. The Bible on the other hand says "*And this is life eternal, that they may know thee— the only true God, and Jesus Christ, whom thou hath sent*" (John 17:3).

Emasculation of Christianity

Islam attacks Christianity with a vengeance. The crux of Christianity centers in the incarnation, the crucifixion, and the resurrection of Jesus Christ from the dead. Islam denies all three of these vital doctrines of the Christian faith. Not only that but they teach that our Holy Bible has been corrupted. The trinity is abominable because God has no wife called Mary, and therefore Jesus Christ is not the Son of God. Christians are polytheists who believe in three gods. Although favoring Jesus with titles such as Word of God, Spirit of God, Messiah, etc., they believe he is only a prophet and a great man, but not the Son of God or Savior or Lord. The Koran is the sourcebook of Muslims for whatever is true about the Bible, Christianity, Christians, and Jesus. Whatever is in the Bible is true only as it does not contradict the writings of the Koran.

The purpose of this chapter is to show a sampling of what the Koran teaches and counter those with what the Bible teaches.

Denial of the Deity of Jesus and the Trinity

The Koran in Surah 3:45—47 says:

> When the angels said: O Marium, surely Allah gives you good news with a Word from Him (of one) whose name is the Messiah, Isa son of Marium, worthy of regard in this world and the hereafter and of those who are made near (to Allah). And he shall speak to the people when in the cradle and when of old age, and (he shall be) one of the good ones. She said: My Lord! when shall there be a son (born) to me, and man has not touched me? He said: Even so, Allah creates what He pleases; when He has decreed a matter, He only says to it, Be, and it is.

This statement affirms the miraculous virgin birth of Jesus Christ, and that Mary is highly regarded by Muslims. Calling him Messiah probably relates to the fact of his virgin birth and prophethood. However, Mohammed and the Koran are anti-Christ in that they deny the deity of Jesus Christ. "They commit blasphemy who say that God is Christ the son of Mary" (Surah 5:19). In Islam the unpardonable sin is called "shirk." To associate the divine nature of God with man is this sin. Thus Islam denies the incarnation of Jesus Christ as the Son of God. To the Muslim mind, Jesus is a created being born without a human father comparable to Adam, who also was created without a human father.

In the Koran, the "People of the Book" (Christians) are warned to commit no excesses in their religion by believing that Jesus is more than a prophet from God.

Surah 4:171 says, "O followers of the Book! do not exceed the limits in your religion, and do not speak (lies) against Allah, but (speak) the truth; the Messiah, Isa son of Marium is only an apostle of Allah and His Word which He communicated to Marium and a spirit from Him; believe therefore in Allah and His apostles, and say not, Three. Desist, it is better for you; Allah is only one God; far be It from His glory that He should have a son, whatever is in the heavens and whatever is in the earth is His, and Allah is sufficient for a Protector.

Muslims erroneously believe the trinity consists of God the father, God the Mother Mary, and as a result of their cohabitation came Jesus Christ, God the Son. They fail to understand the union of three persons, Father, Son, Holy Spirit in one Godhead so that all three persons are one God as to substance.

Crucifixion or Crucifiction?

The key portion of the Koran denying the death of Christ on the cross is Surah 4:156-158 which says:

And for their unbelief and for their having uttered against Marium a grievous calumny. And their saying: Surely we have killed the Messiah, Isa son of Marium, the apostle of Allah; and they did not kill him nor did they crucify him, but it appeared to them so (like Isa) and most surely those who differ therein are only in a doubt about it; they have no knowledge respecting it, but only follow a conjecture, and they killed him not for sure. Nay! Allah took him up to Himself; and Allah is Mighty, Wise.

There is much conjecture as to who died in Jesus' place but the most popular tradition is that Judas Iscariot died on the cross not Jesus. Compare this conjecture with the sure words of Scripture; *"For I delivered unto you first of all that which I also received, how that Christ died for our sins according to the scriptures; and that he was buried, and that he rose again the third day according to the scriptures; And that he was seen of Cephas, then of the twelve: After that, he was seen of above five hundred brethren* at once; of whom the greater part remain unto this present, but some are fallen asleep. After that, he was seen of James; then of all the apostles. And last of of all he was seen of me also, as of one born out of due time (I Corinthians 15:3-8).

Mankind Not Sinful only Weak

Muslims believe that man has a moral weakness rather than a sinful nature. Because of disobedience, Adam and Eve were expelled from the Garden of Eden but not separated from God. Islamic traditions teach that a child is born "naturally inclined toward the true religion, which is understood to be Islam" but is perverted after birth by his environment. According to Islam, man needs laws, direction and community to keep him in the straight way. Since man is not a sinner, there is no need for a Savior. Whereas the Bible speaks forthrightly that man is not weak or sick but is dead in trespasses and sins. *"Wherefore, as by one man sin entered into the world, and death by sin; and so death passed upon all men, for all that have sinned"* (Romans 5:12).

No Sacrifice For Sins

The concept of a sacrifice for sin eludes the Muslim. Yahiya Emerick, a Muslim apologist has this to say:

> Yes, Adam and Eve sinned, the Qur'an says, but God forgave them when they asked for his mercy. No sin was passed on to their descendants. Thus, it is our cumulative faith and actions that determine our salvation. The Qur'an declares that Allah can forgive any sin He wants to, whenever He wants to, and that He has no children or any need for them to act as sacrifices. Certainly God would never allow Himself to be tortured and killed by his creatures before He would forgive them! The Qur'an explains that it is beneath the majesty of God to do such things. It is no sign of love for a Muslim that God would die for him or her. So the doctrines of original sin and the Trinity have no room in Islamic concept of God because Islam asserts that God's power is great enough for Him to forgive anything without requiring His death first.[1]

By contrast the word of God declares:

"For the wages of sin is death; but the gift of God is eternal life through Jesus Christ our Lord" (Romans 6:23). *"For God so loved the world, that he gave his only begotten Son, that whosoever believeth in him should not perish, but have everlasting life"* (John 3:16). *"And almost all things are by the law purged with blood; and without shedding of blood there is no remission (forgiveness)"* (Hebrews 9:22).

Separation of Church (religion) and State

In the area of government and politics, the Bible and the Koran are diametrically opposed. Islam functions as a theocracy similar to the time of Moses. God was the King; Moses His representative. George Braswell, Jr., in his good book, *What You Need to Know About Islam and Muslims,* speaks about how Islam is a theocracy:

> Early Islam took the form of a theocracy. Muhammad, following visions from God, ruled in God's name. What became known as the "The Constitution of Medina" was the blueprint for the community of believers and their relationships with nonbelievers.
>
> The constitution gave Muhammad the power and authority not only to be prophet (which he already had from the revelations from God) but also political leader, judge, worship leader, and commander in chief.[2]

A study of Islam reveals that consistency is one of its hallmarks.

> A gathering of worldwide Islamic leaders in London in 1980 issued a statement for the establishment of an Islamic Order. It cited that only God confers authority on rulers, governments, and institutions, and that an Islamic government must follow the mandatory principles in the Quran and in the traditions. The statement emphasized brotherhood, justice, and consensus. It did not mention individual liberty or political freedom.[3]

Such a mindset on the part of Muslims living in a non-Muslim land produces inevitable tensions.

Render to God What is Caesar's

Hassan al-Banna was one of the key figures in the Muslim Brotherhood Movement in Egypt. His anti-government activities resulted in his death. This man showed the difference between the Islamic and Christian views of government. Al-Banna said the following:

> It is not our fault that (in Islam) politics is part of religion and that Islam includes the rulers and the ruled, for its teaching is not: 'Give to Caesar what is Caesar's and to God what is God's, [sic] but rather: Caesar and what is Caesar's are to the one and only victorious God.[4]

In the Muslim mind, there can be no separation of God and politics. Islam is not only a matter of faith and practice; it is also an identity and a loyalty—for many, an identity and a loyalty that transcend all others.

The U.S. government has been lax in opening the doors of our country to Muslim immigrants even to them from countries considered risky or openly unfriendly to U.S. interests— but also supporters and propagators of radical Islam, or agents of terrorist regimes and organizations.[5] Every person that chooses to be a citizen of the United States of America takes an oath of allegiance:

> I hereby declare an oath, that I absolutely and entirely renounce and abjure all allegiance and fidelity, prince, potentate, state, or sovereignty of whom or which I have heretofore been a subject or citizen; support and defend the Constitution and laws of the United States of America against all enemies; that I will bear the true faith and allegiance to the same; that I will bear arms on behalf of the U. S. when required by the law; that I will take this obligation freely without any mental reservation or purpose or evasion; so help me God.[6]

A true Christian can take this oath with full integrity because he has a double responsibility: a responsibility to God and a responsibility to Caesar (government). Peter teaches us to "submit to every ordinance of man for the Lord's sake: whether it be to the king (government)... For so is the will of God" (I Peter 2:13,4). Recent incidents prove that some Muslims who are American citizens are having difficulties with their loyalties. Sergeant Hasan Akbar, the black American Muslim soldier in Kuwait, rolled grenades into three tents. He rolled a grenade into the tent of two commanding officers with a taunt: "You guys are coming into our countries and you're going to rape our women and kill our children." The two American officers, who had not raped any women or killed any children, died. Why is our government so quiet about this murderer and traitor? The American chaplain that converted to Islam during Desert Storm in Arabia betrayed his oath by spying for the enemy in Guantanomo Bay in Cuba. Another Muslim Air Force enlisted man has been charged with serious espionage that could get him the death penalty. [7]

Plan to Islamize Europe

Countries in Europe who have imported large numbers of Muslims to supplement their labor force are now facing critical challenges. Serge Trifvocic gives startling statistics as to present developments and future Islamic goals:

> In 30 years, the Muslim population of Great Britain rose from 82,000 to 2 million. In Germany, there are 4 million Muslims, mostly Turks, and over 5 million in France, mostly North Africans .... Almost a tenth of all babies born in EU countries are Muslims, and in the moribund Brussels, the figure was over 50 percent. With the expanding numbers and the creation of distinctly Muslim neighborhoods in Western, primarily European cities, the initial detachment of culture from territory has been reversed, and the bold notion of conquest by demographic rather than military means entered the activist's minds. The blueprint was developed over two decades ago, in 1981, when the Third Islamic Summit Conference of Kaaba adopted the "Mecca Declaration." It stated

as follows:
We have resolved to conduct Jihad with all the
means at our disposal so as to free our territory
from occupation. (Whole world is their territory).
We declare that the oppression suffered by Muslim minorities and communities in many countries is a flagrant offense against the rights and
dignity of man.
We appeal to all states in, which there are Islamic
minorities to allow them full liberty.
We are convinced of the need to propagate the
precepts of Islam and its cultural influence in
Muslim societies and throughout the world.[8]

For the serious thinker and anyone concerned about the preservation of our free society the unhindered growth of Muslim
communities in non-Muslim countries causes deep concern.

Eschatology in Islam

It has been my privilege to discuss eschatology with Muslim
friends who were knowledgeable about the teachings and traditions of Islam. As we learned earlier, the Koran states that
Jesus did not die on the cross but was taken to heaven by Allah.
So presently Jesus is in heaven. According to Islamic teaching
in the last days Dajjal, the anti-Christ, will appear. He will gather
an army to fight against God's faithful. None other than Jesus
Christ will save the Muslim cause! I am now quoting from Yahiya
Emerick as he describes the last days:

When the time for the morning prayer arrives,
the Prophet Jesus, who had been saved from
dying on the cross thousands of years before and
had been kept in Paradise by God, will descend
in the midst of Damascus. After joining Muslims
in prayer, he will lead the Mahdi's forces against
the Dajjal's army...
On the battlefield, Jesus will command his troops
to move aside ... Upon seeing Jesus, the Dajjal's
powers will fade and he will make a panicky re-
treat to Palestine.... Jesus will strike down the
Dajjal with a lance, and his reign of tyranny will
be over.[9]

But this is not all. According to Muslim teaching, Jesus will preach to both Jews and Christians resulting in their conversion to Islam. At this time the world will enjoy 40 years of peace during which time Jesus marries, has children and finally dies.[10] Muslims have told me that Jesus will be buried beside Mohammed in Medina. If this is truly a part of Muslim beliefs, I do not know. However, I do know such teaching is false.

Fact Not Fancy

Contrast these fantasies with the powerful inerrant Word of God:

> *"And to you who are troubled rest with us, when the Lord Jesus shall be revealed from heaven with mighty angels, in flaming fire taking vengeance on them that know not God, and that obey not the gospel of our Lord Jesus Christ: who shall be punished with everlasting destruction from the presence of the Lord, and from the glory of his power, when he shall come to be glorified in his saints, and to be admired in all them that believe"* (II Thessalonians 3:7-10).

Yes, there are insuperable differences between Islam and Christianity.

End Notes:

1. Emerick. P. 44.
2. Braswell, George, Jr., *What You Need to Know About Islam and Muslims,* Broadman Holman Publishers, Nashville, TN, 2000, p. 86.
3. Ibid.
4. Zacharias, p. 45.
5. Trifvocic, pp. 264, 265.
6. United States Immigration and Naturalization Service website.
7. Pruden, Wesley, WTW, 9/29—10/5/03, *Christian View of the News.*
8. Trifvocic, p. 264.
9. Emerick, p. 108
10 Ibid.

GOOD NEWS FOR MUSLIMS

Both Islam and Christianity are missionary religions. As such, each is seeking to win converts of the other. Both religions are exclusive, i.e., each claims to be true and reject all others as false. Jesus Christ said, "I am the way, the truth, and the life: no man cometh to the Father, but by me" (John 14:6). Concerning Jesus Christ, C.S. Lewis wrote as follows:

> A man who was merely a man and said the sort of things Jesus said would not be a great moral teacher. He would either be a lunatic—on a level with the man who says he is a poached egg—or else he would be the Devil of Hell. You must make your choice. Either this man was, and is, the Son of God, or else a madman or something worse.[1]

Islam's *shahadah*, reads, "There is no God but Allah, and Mohammed is the messenger of Allah" and this statement is the bedrock belief of Muslims.[2] According to the rules of logic, both of these statements cannot be true. Either Christ is who He says He is, or He is a fake. Likewise Mohammed is the seal of the prophets as he claims, or he is an impostor. Likewise the holy Bible is the eternal word of God, or the holy Koran is the eternal word of Allah. Both cannot be the Word of God. All this talk about one religion being as good as the other or the Allah of the Koran and the Jehovah of the Bible being the same is nonsense.

Compare the Commands

The Bible and the Koran present two different mind sets. First, let us look at the Biblical mind set. In the Bible, Adam and Eve were created in the image of God, i.e., they possessed intelligence [knowledge], volition [will], and emotion [feelings]. Before the Fall, they walked and talked with God. The Bible is "His Story" of providing a way for sinful man to be reconciled to a holy God. The Great Commission [commandment] reads like this: *"Go therefore and make disciples of all nations, baptizing them in the name of the Father, and the Son, and the Holy Spirit, teaching them to observe* (obey) *all that I have commanded you, and lo,*

I am with you always even unto the end of the age" (Matthew 28:19, 20). In another place, Christians are commanded to be witnesses of Christ's suffering, death, and resurrection and to proclaim forgiveness of sins and repentance in His name to all nations (Luke 24:47,48). The Bible extends an invitation to sinful men: *"The Spirit* (Holy Spirit) *and the bride* (the church), *say, Come, let the one who is thirsty come, let the one who wishes take the water of life* (eternal life) *without cost"* (Revelation 22:17). This Gospel is to be taken to the entire world: *"Go ye into all the world and preach the gospel to every creature. He that believeth and is baptized shall be saved; but he that believeth not shall be damned"* (Mark 16:15, 16). No where in the Bible does God force anybody to love Him or to serve Him.

Koran's Command to Fight

At the beginning of Mohammed's ministry in Mecca, he preached to his idolatrous countrymen, to the Jews and to the Christians. During this time, his approach was peaceful and conciliatory. After being rejected by the Meccans, the Jews, and the Christians, he and his followers fled to Medina. Here he was welcomed as a religious, political, and military leader, all in one.

At this time his new religion underwent a drastic change. In Mecca when he was weak, Mohammed fought with words to overcome his adversaries, i.e., the idolaters, the Jews, and the Christians. Now in Medina when he was strong and in control, he began military expeditions in the name of Allah to do by the sword what he could not do by words. Without a doubt, Mohammed was a man of strong conviction believing with all his heart that Allah was the only god, that he was his prophet, and that the Koran was the eternal word of Allah. In the Koran, we find what might be called the Great Commission of Islam: Surah 2.193 says, "And fight with them until there is no persecution, (disbelief) and religion should be only for Allah, but if they desist, then there should be no hostility except against the oppressors."

After subduing the Arabian Peninsula, Mohammed extended an invitation of sorts to the surrounding nations: "Accept Islam by confessing that there is no god but Allah and Mohammed is his prophet." According to Mark Gabriel, Islamic scholar and author, Mohammed gave people who were non-Muslims three choices:

One, They could accept the message of Islam. Two, they could remain Jews or Christians but pay a special tax (jizyah) which is traditionally levied once a year. Three, they could die. Surah 9:29 speaks to the subject. "Fight those who do not believe in Allah, nor in the latter day, nor do they prohibit what Allah and His Apostle have prohibited, nor follow the religion of truth, out of those who have been given the Book, until they pay the tax in acknowledgment of superiority and they are in a state of subjection." The phrase "and feel themselves subdued or in a state of submission" means something like "abject subjection." It carries the idea of someone cowering in fear before a greater power. If abject submission is not achieved, then death follows.[3]

Muslims Are Not Enemies

The great difference between Islam and Christianity is how they view outsiders, i.e., non-Christians and non-Muslims. To the Christian, non-Christians are valuable to God because He loved them so much He sent His Son into the world to save them. If they believe, repent of their sins, and receive God's Son, He gives them the gift of eternal life. If they choose not to believe, then the consequence of their rejection is eternal separation from God. Muslims are not enemies; they are people for whom Christ died and whom He wants to save. However, to the Muslim the unbeliever is the enemy of Allah in that he refuses to submit to Allah and his prophet Mohammed and as such must be killed. I would remind my reader this is not what I think. In Islam the world is divided into the world of *Dar al-Harb* (the world of war, non-Islamic people) and the *Dar al-Islam* (the world of peace, the Muslim world. Bernard Lewis, renowned historian and expert on Islam, explains it succinctly:

> In Muslim tradition, the world is divided into two houses: the House of Islam *(Dar al-Islam)*, in which Muslim governments rule and Muslim law prevails, and the House of War *(Dar al-Harb)*, the rest of the world, still inhabited and, more important, ruled by infidels. The presumption is that the duty of jihad will continue, interrupted

only by truces, until all the world either adopts the Muslim faith or submits to the Muslim rule. Those who fight in the jihad qualify for rewards in both worlds—booty in the one, paradise in the next.[4]

The purpose of Islam is to impose the Islamic faith and rule (shari'a) in all the world. In contrast, the purpose of Christ is to call out of the nations a people of faith for Himself.

Muslim Misconceptions

Most Muslims believe with all their hearts that Islam is far superior to Christianity. This perception is true for several reasons. First, their religion forces an outward morality by outlawing alcohol, dancing, and rock music. However, no religion can take the sin out of sinful hearts, and Muslim countries are not famous for their honesty, helpfulness, and goodness. Corruption is rife from the top to the bottom. Second, most Muslims have no idea what a true Christian is. People who live in the West are considered to be Christians. All people such as Americans, Englishmen, Frenchmen, Germans, are Christians. They are blissfully unaware that the secularists and the humanists hate Christianity and are making every effort to destroy our Biblical heritage. Because of the sinful lifestyles of most Europeans and Americans, a negative idea is associated with the name "Christian." Because of Hollywood, the liquor industry, gambling, and pornography in our country, they think that Christians are immoral people. Ungodly movies and TV programs exported around the world cause Muslims to believe that what they see represents Christian America. In most Islamic countries, Eastern Orthodox and Roman Catholic Christians are numerous and visual. Their lifestyles are everything but godly. Catholics are famous for their drinking, dancing, and carousing. To a Muslim, the worst thing that could happen to their children is for them to become Christians. Most Muslims have never met a real Christian that loves God and lives a holy life.

Evangelizing Muslims

Christians are commanded to go to Muslim nations to preach the Gospel. Most Muslim nations will not let missionaries into their countries to preach. Some countries, like Bangladesh, do let them in but carefully monitor them. God is sending Muslims by the thousands to our country. Born again Christians have a great opportunity not only to tell the Gospel but to also show Muslims what a real true Christian is.

Steps in Evangelizing Muslims

Dr. Mark Gabriel, in his excellent book, *Islam and Terrorism—What the Quran really teaches about Christianity,* violence and the goals of the Islamic jihad, published by Charisma House gives ten commandments for sharing the Gospel with Muslims. I would suggest anyone interested in knowing more about Islam and terrorism read this book.

Make "friends." Most Muslim people living in America do not have any or at least many American friends. Muslim people respond to friendship and hospitality. They would love to come to your home to see what Americans live like. They would enjoy sitting at your table for a meal, however, you should not serve pork. If we are going to evangelize Muslims, the first thing we have to do is to cultivate a friendship. Saying, "Hello. How are you?" is not enough. We need to come along side and get to know him, know his problems, his frustrations, his ambitions, and his fears. We need to offer advice and help, as we are able. He will soon learn that a true Christian is one who is honest, does not drink or gamble, is moral, loves God, and loves his fellowman. This will make a great impress on him. There are not too many people like that in this world.

"Prayer." Pray first that God will give you a Muslim friend. Be on the lookout as Muslims are all around us. Ask him his name and where he is from. Ask about his mother and father and brothers and sisters. Make a point to meet him regularly. Once you make a friendship, begin to pray that God would use you to impact this individual for Christ. Pray for conviction of sin. Pray for spiritual understanding on his part. Pray for wisdom in explaining what you believe and why. God will give you the courage and the wisdom you need.

Share with him the "Word of God." He believes that the Bible is the Word of God and as such he will respect it. A Gospel of Matthew written especially for Muslims is available. It uses the Muslim vocabulary with which he is familiar. A Muslim is very religious and unlike most Americans welcomes spiritual conversations. So don't be shy to talk about subjects such as these: Christ, sin, heaven, and hell. Tell him of your assurance of salvation because our God cannot lie.

"Ask thought-provoking questions." Good questions to ask are: Do you have assurance that God will accept you? What does the Koran say about forgiveness? Is God more concerned with our outward ceremonies or the attitude of our hearts? Do you serve God because you love Him or because you fear Him? Is God able to forgive sins without a sacrifice? Can God lie? Can we trust God to keep His promises?

"Listen attentively." When you ask a question, courtesy requires that you listen to the answer no matter how long it takes. You will be surprised at how much you will learn.

"Present your beliefs openly without apology." State what you believe, clearly and without apology, showing Scripture that supports those teachings. Thus, you place the responsibility for doctrine where it belongs—on the Word of God. Talk about sin and how it affects our lives. Show examples from the daily news. Say, "sin is the biggest problem in our world today. How do we deal with sin?" A person living in sin hates himself. He is an enemy to himself. Most Muslims recognize that they are living in sin, but don't know how to get forgiveness or deliverance. Tell them how Jesus forgives sin and gives victory over sin.

"Reason don't argue." Argument may win a point but lose a hearing. Listen to his objections without getting upset. Don't argue about the trinity or the deity of Christ. Once a Muslim receives Christ he will understand these matters. Keep to the point that he is a sinner and needs forgiveness and assurance from God.

"Never denigrate Mohammed or the Koran." This is very offensive to them as they reverence their prophet and their holy book. We do not appreciate people using the Lord's name in vain and speaking disrespectfully of Christ and the Bible. "He that throws mud loses ground." Preach Christ and the Bible and leave opinions of Mohammed and the Koran to them.

"Respect their customs and sensitivities." Let me mention a few things that will offend your Muslim friend. Do not offend by placing your Bible on the floor or treating it carelessly. They revere their holy book and keep it wrapped in velvet and in an elevated place. Do not speak about sex; it is dirty to Muslims. Do not appear too familiar with the opposite sex. Be discrete and proper in this regard. Do not make jokes about sacred things as prayer, fasting, heaven, hell or God. Do not offer them pork to eat. To them, the pig is an unclean animal and not to be eaten. Of course, do not offer them alcohol in any form. Do not dress immodestly whether you are male or female. Muslims do not like shorts on men or women. Notice how careful their women cover themselves.

"Persevere." Muslims that are confronted with the claims of Christ and the Bible, and the testimony of a true faithful Christian have a lot of rethinking to do. Do not rush them into a decision to believe and accept Christ. Let the Word of God and the Holy Spirit do their work in their hearts. Muslims can be won for Christ. It will require Christians leaving their comfort zones and reaching out to Muslims. Before winning a Muslim to Christ, we must win him to ourselves. They must see in us a reality of the presence of God that they have never seen in a Muslim teacher. It is true that Islam, as a religion, is a threat to our republic. However, individual Muslims are not the enemy. They are enslaved in a powerful religion that refuses to let them go. Only the truth can set them free. *"And ye shall know the truth, and the truth shall make you free"* (John 8:32). God loves the Muslims as much as he loves us. *"But God commended his love toward us, in that, while we were yet sinners, Christ died for us"* (Romans 5:8).[5]

Muslims Can Be Saved

It is not easy to win Muslims to Christ, but it is not impossible. Let me give you a few examples to encourage you. In the course of our mission work, a hard working Muslim man by the name of S. came to work for us. We became good friends. He attended a men's Bible study each Wednesday afternoon and would come and sit at the back to listen to the Word of God. He would shake his head and say *hehh, hehh, hehh.* That means yes. Although S. was illiterate, he was very intelligent. He believed the truth of the Bible that he was a sinner, that Jesus was the Son of God, and died on the cross for his sins and rose from the dead. S. believed and was wonderfully saved. He taught his wife, A. And she also believed and was saved. They were baptized and became charter members of the church. They were insulted and harassed by their neighbors for their Christian faith, but God protected them. They had a large family and all the children believed and were saved. This all took place 40 years ago. S. and A. are now old but their son, Y., is a man of 40 and is an evangelist and pastor. He pastors the church that meets in their village home each Friday. S.'s daughter, K., is married to F., a Muslim convert who preaches the Gospel to Muslim people who visit our hospital. Another son works in our Bible Correspondence School. On a previous trip, I watched K. baptize five Muslims who had believed on Christ.

More recently I received an e-mail from a supporting church in Virginia Beach, VA, that was very encouraging. A Muslim man was in an automobile accident, and the people of the church came to his aid. They helped with the doctor's bill and ministered to him during his time of healing. This Afghani Muslim has been saved and wants to go back to Afghanistan as witness for Christ. Pray for him as American Muslims are threatening to kill him for becoming a Christian.

Heavy Responsibility

In His providence, God is sending the world to our neighborhoods. Are we going to accept the challenge to make friends and share the good news of Christ with our Muslim, Hindu, and Buddhist neighbors? If we fail, God is going to hold us accountable, and their blood will be on our hands.

End Notes

1. C. S. Lewis, *Mere Christianity,* Geoffrey Bles, Ltd, London, England, 1952, p. 41.
2. Anis Shorrosh, *Islam Revealed—A Christian Arab's View of Islam,* Thomas Nelson Publishers, Nashville, TN, 1988, p. 32.
3. Mark Gabriel, *Islam and Terrorism—What the Quran Really Teaches about Christianity, Violence and the Goals of Islamic Jihad,* Charisma House, Lake Mary, FL, 2002, pp. 198—200.
4. Bernard Lewis, pp. 31, 32.
5. Gabriel, pp. 198-200.

The terrorists are quick to confess their hatred of Israel and the Great Satan (United States) that protects it. When confronted with their terrorism, the Islamic terrorists will vehemently blame Israel and the United States as the real culprits. Osama bin Laden accuses Israel of slaughtering Muslims, robbing them of their land, and inflicting all kinds of shame and dishonor on Islam. To understand the tensions and the hatreds that presently exist, it is necessary to get a historical perspective concerning the relationship between Muslims and Jews.

The Media Gets It Wrong

Much research has gone into writing this book. I have read both sides: those championing Islam as a tolerant religion and those exposing it as a threat to the free world. As usual, the media takes the wrong side. The information dispensed by the media is very misleading. The best-selling book, *Islam—A Short History,* by Karen Armstrong, a converted nun, took the country by storm. *The New York Times* had good things to say about the book:

> No religion in the modern world is as feared and misunderstood as Islam. It haunts the popular imagination as an extreme faith that promotes terrorism, authoritarian government, female oppression, and civil war. In *a vital revision of this narrow view of Islam* and a distillation of years of thinking and writing about the subject, Karen Armstrong's short history demonstrates that the world's fastest growing religion is a much more complex phenomenon than its modern fundamentalist strain might suggest.[1]

Islam a Religion of Tolerance

Karen Armstrong goes to much pain to paint Islam as a tolerant, kind religion with "live and let live" as its theme. Let me give you three quotes that show her basic dishonesty in attempting to whitewash Islam:

> Hence Muhammad never asked Jews or Christians to accept Islam unless they particularly wished to do so, because they had received perfectly valid revelations of their own.[2]
>
> The Quran continued to.... urge Muslims to respect the People of the Book.[3]
>
> Smaller Jewish groups.... like Christians enjoyed full religious liberty in the Islamic empires.[4]

This book has been quoted frequently on the PBS special about the life of Muhammad. Michael Elliott, *Islam's Prophet Motive.*[5] This book was also required reading for the freshman class at the University of North Carolina at Chapel Hill, NC, in the fall of 2002.

Why is it that some people insist Islam is tolerant, and other claim it is a religion based on force and coercion? Both sides quote the Koran, which is considered to be the very words of Allah. Along with the Koran, Muslims consider the Hadith, the records of Mohammed's teachings and actions to be authoritative. Since we will be going to these sources to prove our case it is important to know that every true Muslim accepts these teachings without doubt.

The New Prophet on the Block

Mohammed lived in the seventh century. Keep in mind that Jews had been worshipping Jahweh for twenty five hundred years, and the Christians had been following Jesus for six hundred years. But the new prophet on the block came with a powerful message. He said to the Jews and the Christians that there God and the God of Islam are the same. "Our Ilah (God) and your Ilah (God) are the same." (Surah 29:46). The Koran says that Islam came before Judaism or Christianity because it was the religion practiced by Abraham.

> Surah 3:67-68 reads, Ibrahim (Abraham) was neither a Jew nor a Christian, but he was a Muslim...Verily, among mankind who have the best claim to Ibrahim (Abraham) are those who followed him, and this Prophet (Muhammad) and those who have believed (Muslims).

How could this be? According to Islam, the Jews and the Christians did receive earlier revelations from Allah, but they had corrupted their scriptures and were no longer worshipping Allah properly, so Allah had to send a fresh revelation by way of Mohammed. According to Islam, the Koran canceled out Christianity and Judaism and brought people back to the one true religion practiced by Father Abraham, i.e., Islam.

This radical teaching must have been a shock to the Jews and Christians of Arabia of the seventh century. In a nutshell, Mohammed, challenged these two historical religions with several claims: Islam claimed to worship the same God as Jews and Christians; Islam has superceded Judaism and Christianity; Mohammed claimed to be the final prophet of Allah; and Islam demanded obedience and acceptance.

Islam Both Tolerant & Aggressive

As we learned in the study of the life of Mohammed, his life can be divided into two phases: the tolerant years in Mecca and the aggressive years in Medina. Mark Gabriel explains his tolerant years simply and eloquently:

> Muhammad was living in Mecca when he first began to receive revelations in 610 A.D. At this time, he was a preacher, trying to win people to Islam by being nice. Even after he and his followers were persecuted and moved to the nearby city of Medina in 622 A.D., Muhammad continued to preach a positive message for about a year, hoping to attract people to Islam that way. Surah 2:256 says, "Let there be no compulsion in religion: Truth stands out clear from Error: whoever rejects Evil and believes in Allah has grasped the most trustworthy hand-hold that never breaks. And Allah hears and knows all things." The verse essentially says, "You can't force anybody to change their religion. The right way should be obvious." People who say Islam is a religion of peace point to this verse. However, they need to take into account that this verse was only an early installment of the revelations of Muhammad received regarding those who rejected Islam.[6]

Mohammed was presenting a peaceful front at this time—a good strategy because he had only a few followers, and they were all very vulnerable. But Islam did not stay weak. The new prophet had worked hard to gain approval of the Jews both in Mecca and Medina. Don Richardson in his powerful expose' of the Koran and Islam brings some interesting insights into Mohammed's dealing with the Jews of Medina:

> Arabs in Medina were asking Jews for their honest evaluation of Mohammed. Medinan Jews were freely offering their opinions. Little did they know that exercising the freedom of speech they had always enjoyed prior to Mohammed's arrival would seal the doom of many of them.[7]

After establishing himself as undisputed leader of Medina, Mohammed ratified the Constitution of Medina, a seemingly benign treaty with both pagans and Jews in Medina. Mohammed was the sole arbitrator of disputes. The treaty bound all parties to peaceful co-existence.[8] As expected, the treaty was violated. The man responsible for mediating the dispute violated his rule as mediator and declared the Constitution of Medina no longer valid and declared war on the Medinan Jews.[9]

Muslim historian Maxime Rodison and Ibn Warrick, an apostate Muslim author of *Why I Am Not a Muslim,* as well as many others record the atrocities Mohammed committed against the Banu Qaynuaq Jews and the Banu Qurayza Jews. These sources describe Mohammed himself presiding over the beheading of at least 500 Jewish men. They were buried in a long ditch they dug for themselves. Their wives and daughters were sold for sex slaves and boys for labor.[10] From that day to this, unbridled hatred characterizes the feeling Muslims and Jews have for one another.

Abrogation a Key Islamic Doctrine

The doctrine of "abrogation" looms large in the Koran and in Islam. Surah 2:106 says that "Whatever communications We abrogate or cause to be forgotten, We bring one better than it or like it. Do you not know that Allah has power over all things?" Allah causes some parts of the Koran to be abrogated. The definition of "abrogate" means to "abolish by authoritarian action," "to treat as nonexistent" or to "nullify". Verses that are "better" or "similar" replace these abrogated verses. The practical application of this principle is that when there is a contradiction between two verses in the Koran, the newer revelation overrides the previous revelation. Then the new cancels the old. You can still read the words, "There is no compulsion in religion," in the Koran, but they no longer have authority because Surah 2:193 says, "And fight with them until there is no presecution, and religion should be only for Allah, but if they desist, then there should be no hostility except against oppressors." So the "no compulsion in religion" verse has been *mansookh* (canceled) by revelations that came later.[11]

Professor Gabriel helps us understand how the Muslims interpret the Koran in this way:

> This principle of abrogation is known in Arabic as *nasikh*. It means that Allah led Muhammad in a progressive revelation. Many copies of the Quran have a table that shows whether a surah is from Mecca or Medina in order to help readers know which is a newer revelation. Even Quranic history shows that *nasikh* is valid. If there were no *nasikh*, then Muhammad's followers would have stayed with tolerant Meccan ideals. There would have been no jihad and no Islamic military to conquer land, and people all over the world. Islam would never have left Arabia.[12]

Jewish complaints Against the Koran

The Jews and the Christians gloried in a God that changes not and in their holy Scriptures that no man dare change. When they witnessed Mohammed's Koran and its doctrine of abrogation, they quickly pointed out the discrepancies. "How can this be of God? What God changes His mind?" Their complaints are mentioned in Surah 16:101,

"And when We change (one) communication for (another) communication, and Allah knows best what He reveals, they say: You are only a forger. Nay, most of them do not know." In the next verse, Allah told Mohammed how to answer these accusations. Surah 16: 102 reads, "Say: The Holy spirit has revealed it from your Lord with the truth, that it may establish those who believe and as a guidance and good news for those who submit." In other words, Allah told Muhammad to simply say that the Koran is true, it came from God, and it is for the benefit of those who believe it. This was the answer about why some new revelations were contradicting some old revelations.[13]

Kind Words for the Jews

The Koran has favorable things to say about the Jews. The Jews are Allah's only chosen people. Surah 2:47 says, "O children of Israel! call to mind My favor which I bestowed on you and that I made you excel the nations."

Allah protected the Jews when they were living as strangers in a foreign land. Surah 28:4-6 says, "Surely Firon (Pharoah) exalted himself in the land and made its people into parties, weakening one party from among them; he slaughtered their sons and let their women live; surely he was one of the mischiefmakers. And We desired to bestow a favor upon those who were deemed weak in the land, and to make them the Imams, and to make them the heirs, And to grant them power in the land, and to make Firon and Haman and their hosts see from them what they feared."

Allah chose all His prophets from the Jewish people. Surah 5:20 reads, And when Musa said to his people: O my people! remember the favor of Allah upon you when He raised prophets among you and made you kings and gave you what He had not given to any other among the nations."

Allah would be kind to Jews and Christians who believe in one God and performed good works. Surah 2:62 says, "Surely those who believe, and those who are Jews, and the Christians, and the Sabians, whoever believes in Allah and the Last day and does good, they shall have their reward from their Lord, and there is no fear for them, nor shall they grieve."

From these surahs it is evident that at one stage in his ministry Mohammed looked with favor on the Jews and Christians. Remember that all these surahs are Meccan revelations and have been abrogated by later Medinan revelations. The new revelations brought bad happenings to the Jews.

When confronted with the teachings of Mohammed, the Jews first listened carefully. Soon it was evident to them that this prophet's teaching, though using the names and histories found in the Old Testament scriptures, were full of discrepancies. The Jews began to mock Mohammed and asked for signs. To make a long story short, relations between Mohammed and the Jews deteriorated quickly and dramatically.

Cursed Be The Jews

Mohammed reacted to their rejection by receiving new revelations from Gabriel. The five kind words Mohammed spoke about the Jews were reversed. Note the five reversals: Allah cursed the Jewish people because of their transgressions. Surah 5:78 says, "Those who disbelieved from among the children of Israel were cursed by the tongue of Dawood and Isa, son of Marium; this was because they disobeyed and used to exceed the limit."

Allah transformed Jews into monkeys and pigs as punishment for their wrongdoing. Surah 7:166 says, "Therefore when they revoltingly persisted in what they had been forbidden, We said to them: Be (as) apes, despised and hated."

Allah condemns the Jews for killing the prophets. Surah 2:91 says, "And when it is said to them, Believe in what Allah has revealed, they say: We believe in that which was revealed to us; and they deny what is besides that, while it is the truth verifying that which they have. Say: Why then did you kill Allah's Prophets before if you were indeed believers?"

Islam is the final religion and the Koran is the last testament: therefore, Jews and Christians must convert. Surah 3:85 says, "And whoever desires a religion other than Islam, it shall not be accepted from him, and in the hereafter he shall be one of the losers."

The Jewish people corrupted the books of God. Surah 2:75 says, "Do you then hope that they would believe in you, and a party from among them indeed used to hear the Word of Allah, then altered it after they had understood it, and they know (this)."

The Corruption of the Scriptures

During my ministry to Muslims, I kept hearing that our scriptures had been corrupted. This, of course, is a serious charge and as such should be backed up by ample proof. I asked my Muslim friends making these accusations several questions: who was the culprit that did this dastardly deed of corrupting the very Word of God? Where are the original, uncorrupted copies? When did this corruption take place? Would you please show me what part is corrupt and what part is pure? Of course, they had no answers. Where are the originals? "They just disappeared," they said. They have nothing to show what the original books said or when the corruption happened only that it was long before the days of Mohammed. They can't say who changed it or what they changed. There is absolutely no proof at all.

Mark Gabriel makes some interesting comments on this subject:

> "Muslim scholars theorize that Christians took out the parts of the New Testament that prophesied Muhammad would come. They say that Christians added in parts about the Trinity, Jesus being God's son, Jesus dying on the cross and salvation by the blood of Jesus. For the Old Testament, they say that the Jews took out the parts that hurt the reputation of the Jews, especially parts about them killing the prophets and being turned into monkeys and pigs a punishment. Muslim scholars also say that the differences between the stories in the Quran and the Old Testament were due to the Jews changing their Scriptures."[13]

Enmity Toward Jews Escalates

Mohammed's enmity toward the Jews continued to increase. The following verses from the Koran form the basis of Islam's hatred of the Jews.

The Koran says the Jews are the greatest enemies of Islam. Surah 5:82 says, Certainly you will find the most violent of people in enmity for those who believe (to be) the Jews and those who are polytheists, and you will certainly find the nearest in friendship to those who believe (to be) those who say: We are Christians; this is because there are priests and monks among them and because they do not behave proudly."

The Koran says that Jewish people do not love Muslims and will not love a Muslim until he converts to Judaism. Surah 2:120 says "And the Jews will not be pleased with you, nor the Christians until you follow their religion. Say: Surely Allah's guidance, that is the (true) guidance. And if you follow their desires after the knowledge that has come to you, you shall have no guardian from Allah, nor any helper.

The Koran says that Jews start wars and cause trouble in the earth. Surah 5:64 says "And the Jews say: The hand of Allah is tied up! Their hands shall be shackled and they shall be cursed for what they say. Nay, both His hands are spread out, He expends as He pleases; and what has been revealed to you from your Lord will certainly make many of them increase in inordinacy and unbelief; and We have put enmity and hatred among them till the day of resurrection; whenever they kindle a fire for war Allah puts it out, and they strive to make mischief in the land; and Allah does not love the mischief-makers."

The Koran condemns both Jews and Christians for saying Allah has a son. Surah 9:30 says "And the Jews say: Uzair is the son of Allah; and the Christians say: The Messiah is the son of Allah; these are the words of their mouths; they imitate the saying of those who disbelieved before; may Allah destroy them; how they are turned away!"

The Koran claims that Jews call Ezra the son of God (which they don't).

The Koran condemns Jews and Christians for saying they are children of God. In Islam it is blasphemy to say, "I am a child of God." Surah 5:18 says And the Jews and the Christians say: We are the sons of Allah and His beloved ones. Say: Why does He then chastise you for your faults? Nay, you are mortals from among those whom He has created, He forgives whom He pleases and chastises whom He pleases; and Allah's is the kingdom of the heavens and the earth and what is between them, and to Him is the eventual coming."

The Koran says the Jews are cursed because they accuse Allah of having a weak hand. Surah 5:64 says "And the Jews say: The hand of Allah is tied up! Their hands shall be shackled and they shall be cursed for what they say. Nay, both His hands are spread out, He expends as He pleases; and what has been revealed to you from your Lord will certainly make many of them increase in inordinacy and unbelief; and We have put enmity and hatred among them till the day of resurrection; whenever they kindle a fire for war Allah puts it out, and they strive to make mischief in the land; and Allah does not love the mischief-makers.

The Koran says that Jews love this present life of this world and do not care about things of eternity. Surah 2:96 says "And you will most certainly find them the greediest of men for life (greedier) than even those who are polytheists; every one of them loves that he should be granted a life of a thousand years, and his being granted a long life will in no way remove him further off from the chastisement."

The Koran says that Jewish people claim to have killed the Messiah. Surah 4:157 says "And their saying: Surely we have killed the Messiah, Isa son of Marium, the apostle of Allah; and they did not kill him nor did they crucify him, but it appeared to them so (like Isa) and most surely those who differ therein are only in a doubt about it; they have no knowledge respecting it, but only follow a conjecture, and they killed him not for sure According to the above points, the Koran concluded that the Jewish people were no longer the chosen people of Allah."

The Koran claims that the followers of Islam were now the chosen people whose responsibility was to protect the true religion. Surah 3:110 says "You are the best of the nations raised up for (the benefit of) men; you enjoin what is right and forbid the wrong and believe in Allah; and if the followers of the Book had believed it would have been better for them; of them (some) are believers and most of them are transgressors."

Words of hatred soon turned into evil actions.[14]

Islam alone Must Reign

Islam is incompatible with any other religion. Surah 9:14,15 says, "Fight them, Allah will punish them by your hands and bring them to disgrace, and assist you against them and heal the hearts of a believing people. And remove the rage of their hearts; and Allah turns (mercifully) to whom He pleases, and Allah is Knowing, Wise." According to their holy book, the Koran, all faiths but Islam must be destroyed. Surah 8:39 says, "And fight with them until there is no more persecution and religion should be only for Allah; but if they desist, then surely Allah sees what they do." The word for "persecution" is *fitnah* (disbelief and polytheism), i.e., worshipping others beside Allah. [15]

Jews returned to their homeland in 1948. It is natural and right for them to want their own nation. Of course, in a matter so immense as returning millions of Jews to their homeland some injustices occurred. Arab people were driven from their homes and farms. However, in my observation of the present Israeli-Arab confrontation, the Jews are not the aggressors but are the victims of Islamic revenge. After 1400 years, they still hate the Jews for their refusal to acknowledge their seventh century visionary, Mohammed, to be the Prophet of Allah.

End Notes

1. Armstrong, Karen, *Islam, A Short History*, Random House, New York, 2002, Blurb on back cover.
2. Ibid., p. 10
3. Ibid. p. 21
4. Ibid.
5. Time, December 23, 2002, p. 76.
6. Gabriel, Islam and the Jews, p. 46.
7. Richardson, Don, *Secrets of the Koran —Revealing Insights into Islam's Holy Book,* Regal Books, Ventura, CA, 2003, p. 36.
8. Ibid.
9. Ibid. p. 48.
10. Rodison, Maxime, *Muhammad,* Pantheon Books, New York, 1971, p. 213 and Warraq, Ibn, *Why I Am Not A Muslim,* Prometheus Books, Amherst, NJ, 1995, p.96.
11. Gabriel, p. 47.
12. Ibid., pp. 48, 49.
13. Ibid., p. 94.
14. Ibid., p. 98—100.
15. Ibid., p. 104.
16. Ibid., p. 46.

Our government, academia, the media, and the market place bend over backwards to avoid being accused of favoring the majority. In fact, we favor the minorities in our midst. In our society, being a white, born again Christian male makes it more difficult to get a job, or to be accepted by a prestigious university. The above qualifications make it next to impossible for such a person to be on the Supreme Court of the United States. The cards are stacked in favor of the non-Caucasians, non-Christians living in our midst. The blatant inequality of this favoritism is being challenged today but with not much success.

What is the Motivation?

What is the basis or motivation of favoring the minority while denying the majority? The answer is multiculturalism, diversity, pluralism and tolerance. The point is to penalize this generation of white males for the sins of past generations. Political correctness demands unquestioning acceptance of other worldviews as of equal validity. Is it not strange that Christians are vilified for claiming that Jesus Christ is the way, the truth, and the life, and no man comes to the Father except by Him? And yet Muslims can say the *shahadah*, "There is no god but Allah and Mohammed is his prophet" without complaint?

America has been blessed because she has received immigrants from around the world integrating them into a free society with no limits to those willing to work. The Irish, the Poles, the Germans, the Italians, the Japanese, the Chinese, the Koreans, and to some extent the Hispanics have come and melted into our American system. For the most part, Muslims tend to cluster together preferring their culture to ours. Detroit, Los Angeles, and New York have areas that are completely dominated by Muslims. That was not the way our system was supposed to work. In spite of their aloofness, America still welcomes them, protects them, and gives them all the benefits our society offers. Thank God in America there are no second-class citizens. If Muslims take over America, it will be a sad day not only for Christians and Jews, but also for the liberal free-thinkers, whether they be atheists, agnostics, humanists, or whatever. All the people of our country will have learned too late what Islam does to all who will not submit to Allah and his seventh century prophet.

Guidelines for People of the Book

The purpose of this book is to warn Americans of what could happen if Islam gains control of our country. Historically, when Islam gains control of a country, its Christian and Jewish inhabitants face three choices: "convert to Islam, pay the tax to the Muslim authority and remain in their faith, or be killed." The guidelines as to how Muslims would treat Jews and Christians were finalized during the caliphate of Umar ibn al Khattab, who was the second caliph.[1]

Mark Gabriel, a converted Muslim and previous professor of Islamic History at Al-Azha University in Cairo, in his excellent book, *Islam and the Jews—the Unfinished Battle,* published by Charisma House has organized the Guidelines of the People of the Book by subjects. With their permission I would like to share them with you.

Showing deference to Muslims
In every situation the People of the Book must defer to Muslims such as standing in their presence, riding donkeys, not horses and riding side saddle, and not building their houses higher than Muslims' houses.
Not offending Muslims.
People of the book could not drink alcohol in the presence of a Muslim, must keep their pigs hidden, bury their dead at night, and not mourn publicly for their dead.

Practicing their religion
In the Jewish synagogues or Christian churches, people were not allowed to raise their voices loud enough to be heard outside the building. People of the Book were not allowed to try to convert Muslims away from Islam.

Law, government, military
People of the Book were prohibited from holding high positions in the Islamic government, from serving in the military, carrying weapons, or from testifying against a Muslim in court.

Special Clothing

People of the Book had to wear special clothing and special colors that identified them as non-Muslims. Christians wore blue; Jews wore yellow; Samaritans wore red. Both men and women wore these colors.

The attitude behind these rules is that People of the Book were impure, filthy infidels, like a disease. Muslims should not have contact with them. Leaders among the Christians and the Jews were responsible for enforcing these rules. If these guidelines were violated, the guilty party would be taken to Islamic court and punishment would be decided there.[2]

In light of the above guidelines it is quite interesting to read an AP news article entitled *Civil Rights a Top Priority for Muslims in This Election:* by Rachel Zoll of the AP:

In 2000, many Muslims made their first unified endorsement in a presidential race, backing George W. Bush thinking he would take a harder line against Israel...and protect the rights of immigrants facing deportation. Muslims say they were disappointed on both counts. Now feeling the additional sting of being scrutinized in the domestic hunt for terrorists, they are mobilizing to express their anger at the polls in 2004.

National Muslim leaders announced plans to register 1 million Muslim voters and make civil rights a top issue in any endorsement of a presidential candidate.

After the September 11, 2001, attacks, Bush won points with American Muslims by visiting a mosque and declaring Islam a peaceful religion. But since then, the federal government has detained hundreds of immigrants, shut down U.S. Muslim charities suspected of terrorist ties, and gained broad new powers to monitor citizens under the U.S. Patriot Act. The Bush administration said these moves have been crucial for U.S. security. American Muslims say they are being scapegoated [3]

Propagandists Par Excellence

American Muslims are struggling to disassociate Islam from the terrorist movement. Mahdi Bray, a black Muslim who was formerly a Baptist, is described in the Bluefield, WV Daily Telegraph as "pacing the floor, hands in motion, preaching with righteous fervor" saying, "We have nothing to be ashamed of. All our religion has to offer America is good—our ethics, our values, our beliefs." The man must be blind to conditions in Saudi Arabia, Iran, and Sudan. These are the countries being ruled by people sharing his ethics, his values, and his beliefs. In a later chapter, we will detail these conditions. In the article above, speaking of the U.S. Patriot Act, Raeed N. Tayeh of the Muslim American Society says, "We see that our rights seem to be eroding: They're raiding Muslim organizations, they're raiding people's home, they're taking people's property, and it doesn't seem reasonable."

In most Muslim countries today the guidelines mentioned above are not in effect. When Mark Gabriel taught Islamic history in Egypt, he said his Muslim students "were very comfortable with the guidelines for ruling non-Muslims." Most students complained, "Look how far we have fallen. The Christians in Egypt are not following these rules. Our Muslim leaders are not strong enough to stand up for Islam." "They longed for the past to be real in the present."[4]

After living in a Muslim country for seventeen years and observing the treatment of non-Muslims, I can truthfully say that non-Muslims are indeed second-class citizens. Few amenities or privileges are theirs. Civil rights! Are you kidding?

End Notes:
1. Gabriel, p. 121.
2. Ibid., pp. 122-125.
3. *Voice in the Wilderness,* Asheville, NC, August, 2003.
4. Gabriel, p. 125.

BATTLE OF THE BOOKS

Any serious discussion of Islam and Christianity will eventually center in the two holy books that support these religions: the Holy Koran and the Holy Bible. The heart of Islam is the Koran just like the heart of Christianity is the Bible. For any claim to be valid it must stand the test of examination. The truth test of correspondence to reality and the test of coherence to reasonable logical thought must be brutally applied. *"The words of the Lord are pure words: as silver tried in a furnace of earth, purified seven times. Thou shalt keep them, 0 Lord, thou shall preserve them from this generation forever"* (Psalm 12:6,7). *"Sanctify them through thy truth: thy word is truth'?* (John 17:17). The Bible is not on trial. It has been tried and proven. Unbelieving scholars have done their best to destroy its credibility yet the Bible stands.

Fate of Those Who Dared To Question

Islam on the other hand makes great claims for their Koran but woe to the scholars who dare raise a question. In 1972, during the renovation of the Great Mosque of Sana'a, ancient Arabic documents and texts were discovered. Let me quote Ravi Zacharias on what happened to the Muslim scholars who critically studied these texts and dared to publish their findings.

> Notable scholars as Ali Dashti from Iran; Nasr Abu Zaid, Egyptian professor of Arabic; Pakistani scholar Fazlur Rahman; Egyptian journalist Farag Foda; Algerian professor of law at the Umversity of Paris Mohammed Arkoun; and Egyptian government minister and university professor Taha Hussein voiced some honest concerns about the texts and their meanings. These devout Muslim men have paid dearly for questioning the authenticity of the primary sources. Ali Dashti mysteriously disappeared during the revolution in Iran. Abu Zaid was branded apostate and forced to flee the country with his wife (she would not have been permitted to remain with him once he was branded apostate). Farag Foda was assassinated,

and so runs the list of those silenced by fear or death.[1]

Thankfully we still live in a country where one can seek the truth and speak the truth without fear of repercussion. Should Islam gain control of this country all dissent would be brutally crushed. So let us take a look at the Koran and its claims.

Contrast between the Bible and the Koran

The Bible begins with eternity and ends with eternity. *"In the beginning God created the heaven and the earth"* (Genesis 1:1). It ends with the redeemed of all ages along with myriads of angels gathered before Him that sits on the throne and the Lamb saying, *"Worthy is the Lamb that was slain to receive power, and riches, and wisdom, and honour, and glory, and blessing... Blessing, and honour, and glory, and power, be unto him that sitteth on the throne, and unto the Lamb forever and ever"* (Revelation 5:12-13). The Bible begins with creation and ends with a recreation. *"And I saw a new heaven and a new earth: for the first heaven and the first earth were passed away"* (Revelation 21:1).

The Bible can be summed up in two words: sin and redemption. Adam and Eve chose to doubt God and believe the Devil. Their sin led to alienation, which necessitated a Redeemer. In Genesis 3:15 God promised a Saviour: *"And I will put enmity between thee and the woman, and between thy seed and her seed; it shall bruise thy head, and thou shalt bruise his heel."* The whole Bible is the outworking of that promise through Abraham, Moses, David, the prophets, and finally the promised Messiah.

In contrast, the Koran starts like this:

> [1.1] All praise is due to Allah, the Lord of the Worlds. [1..2] The Beneficent, the Merciful.
> [1.3] Master of the Day of Judgment.
> [1.4] Thee do we serve and Thee do we beseech for help. [1.5] Keep us on the right path.
> [1.6] The path of those upon whom Thou hast bestowed favors. Not (the path) of those upon whom Thy wrath is brought down, nor of those who go astray.

For those of you who will never buy a Koran and read it for yourselves, let me give you a sample of how it begins and a sample of how it ends. First the beginnmg.

> The Cow
> In the name of Allah, the Beneficent, the Merciful
>
> [2.1] Alif Lam Mim.
> [2.2] This Book, there is no doubt in it, is a guide to those who guard (against evil).
> [2.3] Those who believe in the unseen and keep up prayer and spend out of what We have given them.
> [2.4] And who believe in that which has been revealed to you and that which was revealed before you and they are sure of the hereafter.
> [2.5] These are on a right course from their Lord and these it is that shall be successful.
> [2.6] Surely those who disbelieve, it being alike to them whether you warn them; or do not warn them; will not believe.
> [2.7] Allah has set a seal upon their hearts and upon their hearing and there is a covering over their eyes, and there is a great punishment for them.
> [2.8] And there are some people who say: We believe in Allah and the last day; and they are not at all believers.
> [2.9] They desire to deceive Allah and those who believe; and they deceive only themselves and they do not perceive.
> [2.10] There is a disease in their hearts, so Allah added to their disease and they shall have a painful chastisement because they lied.
> [2.11] And when it is said to them, Do not make mischief in the land, they say: We are but peacemakers.
> [2;12] Now surely they themselves are the mischief makers, but they do not perceive.
> [2..13] And when it is said to them: Believe as the people believe they say:
> Shall we believe as the fools believe? Now surely

they themselves are the fools, but theydo not know.

The first surah or chapter goes in like vein for 286 verses! The arrangement of the Koran is by the length of the surah or chapter. The longest is first and the shortest is last. Now we want to see how it ends.

> The People
> In the name of Allah, the Beneficent, the Merciful,
> [114.1] Say: I seek refuge in the Lord of men,
> [114.2] The King of men, [114.3] The God of men,
> [114.4] From the evil of the whisperings of the slinking (Shaitan),
> [114.5] Who whispers into the hearts of men,
> [114.6] From among the jinn and the men.
> Fini!

From this little demonstration one can see there is a vast contrast in the arrangement, the style, the content, and the purpose of the two books. The purpose of the Bible is found in John 20:31, *"But these are written, that ye might believe that Jesus is the Christ, the Son of God; and that believing ye might have life through his name."* According to Mark Gabriel, Muslim by birth, an Arabic and Islamic professor by profession, and a Christian by choice, informs us of the purpose of the Koran as follows:

> The final revelations of the Quran commanded Muslims to destroy any form of religion that was not submitted to Allah. It became their duty to go and kill Jews, Christians and any other non-Muslims. The goal. was to make Islam the only religion controlling the world. The only way to stop being the object of attack is to stop worshipping other gods, beside Allah. Surah 8:39 "And fight with them until there is no more persecution and religion should be only for Allah; but if they desist, then surely Allah sees what they do.[2]

Now you know why I entitled this book, *The Peril of Islam-Telling the Truth.*

The Word in Bible and the Word in Islam

E. Stanley Jones said there were three types of religion in the world. First, a religion in which the word made word i.e., God revealing Himself through a book such as in Islam. Second, word made law in which God reveals Himself in a set of rules to be followed such as Judaism's Old Testament. Third, the word made flesh in Jesus Christ as in Christianity. Jones goes on to say, "If humans were libraries, the best way to communicate with them would be through a book. If humans were constitutions and by-laws, they would respond to a set of laws. Because we are human, God chose to make the word flesh.[3]

Anis Shorrosh, a Christian Arab and a Southern Baptist evangelist, has insightful words about the way Muslims view their book, the Koran.

> The Muslims seem to believe that in the beginning was the "Word" and the "Word" became a "Book"! Muslims assert that Allah has revealed himself most clearly in a book, not in Muhammad the person: Indeed, according to my count, the word "book" occurs 259 times in the Quran: In contra-distinction, Christians believe the "Word" became a human being. "In the beginning was the Word, and the Word was with God, and the Word was God.... And the Word was made flesh, and dwelt among us, (and we beheld his glory as of the only begotten of the Father) full of grace and truth" (John 1:1, 14).[4]

Infuence of the Bible Versus the Influence of the Koran

People do live according to their beliefs. Mothers in India cast their babies to the crocodiles because they are following their beliefs. Hindu families burned widows (a custom called suttee) along with their husbands because they were following their beliefs. Five Christian missionaries in 1953 sacrificed their lives to reach the Auca tribe for Christ. They were just living according to their beliefs. On September 11, 19 Muslim hijackers devastated the World Trade Centers killing themselves and thousands of innocent people because they were following the teachings of their holy book and following the directions of their champion, Osama bin Laden.

History is a wonderful teacher if we would only listen. It has already been mentioned in this book that the sons of Ishmael went to Africa seeking slaves. Christian missionaries were late coming to Africa, but when they did come their impact was nothing less than phenomenal. These Christian missionaries opposed slavery. Robert Moffatt led the way in 1816. Mary Slessor followed in the 1840's and David Livingston in the 1850's. By the year 1904, million of Africans were Christians. In 2000, there were 300 million African Christians.[5]

In this history lesson we learn that "And ye shall know the truth, and the truth shall make you free" (John 8:32). The Muslim teachers had a problem. The Koran did not authorize them to oppose slavery, but rather encouraged this abominable practice. On the other hand, Christian missionaries fought to eradicate the horrible slave trade. Don Richardson points out the great difference the truth of freedom brought to Africa:

> Consider that all 300 million Christians in sub-Sahara Africa would likely be Muslims today had not the Koran itself prevented Muslim Mullah's from opposing Islam's slave trade in Africa. Thus did Islam waste the 1,000 year head start Christianity allowed it to have in black Africa.[6]

Grandiose Claims for the Holy Koran

Muslims are high on their Koran. Without going into detail let me mention a few of their claims. One, the Koran claims to be inspired of Allah. Surah 39: 1, 2 says, "The Revelation of the Book is from Allah, the Mighty, the Wise. Surely We have revealed to you the Book with the truth, therefore serve Allah, being sincere to Him in obedience."

The Bible also claims to be inspired of God. *"All scripture is given by inspiration." (God breathed) of God..."* (II Timothy 3:16). *"For the prophecy came not in old times by the will of man: but holy men of God spake as they were moved by the Holy Ghost"* (II Peter 1:21). *"God, who at sundry times and in divers manners spake in times past unto the fathers by the prophets, Hath in these last days spoken unto us by His Son"* (Hebrews 1:1).

Two, the Koran is inerrant (without error) and eternal. Surah 18:1 says, "(All) praise is due to Allah, Who revealed the Book to His servant and did not make in it any crookedness." Surah 43:3, 4 says, "Surely We have made it an Arabic Quran that you may understand. And surely it is in the original of the Book with Us truly elevated, full of wisdom."

The Bible also claims eternality for itself. *"Forever, O Lord, thy word is settled* (established) *in heaven"* (Psalm 119:89). *"For verily I say unto you, Till heaven and earth pass, one jot or one tittle shall in no wise pass from the law, till all be fulfilled"* (Matthew 5:18). *"In the beginning was the Word, and the Word was with God and the Word was God. The same was in the beginning with God"* (John I: 1 ,2).

Three, the Koran is God's final revelation to mankind. Surah 10:37 says, "And this Quran is not as such as could be forged by those besides Allah, but it is a verification of that which is before it and a clear explanation of the book, there is no doubt in it, from the Lord of the worlds."

Please note that the Bible claims to have all that is necessary for a wholesome life. *"All scripture is profitable for doctrine, for reproof, for correction, for instruction in righteousness: That the man of God may be thoroughly furnished unto all good works"* (II Timothy 3: 16, 17).

There are many more claims made for the glorious Koran, such as the unity of the Koran, its scientific accuracy, perfect preservation, and unique literary style, but let me share one more claim: lives changed by the Koran. Muslim scholar Ajijola waxes eloquent describing lives and cultures changed by Islam:

> The transformation wrought by the Holy Quran is unparalleled in the history of the world and thus its claim to being unique stands as unchallenged today as it did thirteen centuries ago... No faith ever imparted such a new life to its votaries on such a wide scale—a life affecting all branches of human activity; a transformation of the individual, of the family, of the society, of the nation, of the country; and awakening material as well as moral, intellectual as well as spiritual. The Quran effected a transformation of humanity from Its lowest depth of degradation to the highest pinnacle of civilization within an

incredible short time where centuries of refor-
mation had proved fruitless.[7]

Does this correspond to reality? Let the reader be the judge.
There is much to be said on the subject of the battle of the
books. For any one interested in a wealth of fascinating reading, I would urge him or her to get *Answering Islam—The Crescent in Light of the Cross* by Norman Geisler and Abdul Saleed.

More Sure Word of Prophecy

Nothing differentiates the Bible from the Koran as much as
fulfilled prophecy. Let me give you just one example of the
Koran's prophecy. Surah 30:2-4 says, "The Romans are vanquished, In a near land, and they, after being vanquished, shall
overcome, Within a few years. Allah's is the command before
and after; and on that day the believers shall rejoice." This is
the example of prophecy given by those defending the Koran.

In contrast to this weak, ambivolent prophecy from the Koran, think with me of the fulfilled prophecy concerning Jesus
Christ. One, Genesis 3:15 tells us He will be a seed of the woman
(a human being), that He will bruise the serpent's (Satan) head,
and Satan will bruise His heel. Two, Genesis 12:2, 3 tells us that
it was through Abraham the blessings would come. Three, Genesis 49:10 tells us that the Messiah would be of the tribe of Judah.
Four, Matthew 1:1 tells us that the Savior will be the son of
David. Not only this but it tells us in Isaiah 7:14 that He shall be
born of a virgin, in Michah 5:2, that He shall be born in
Bethlehem, in Isaiah 53; 5, that He was wounded to heal our
sins, in Psalm 22:16, that they would put nails in His hands and
feet, in Daniel 9:25, 26, the year the Messiah will be cut off, and
in Psalm 16:10, that our Savior will rise from the dead. Since all
these prophecies have been literally fulfilled, I am full of confi-
dence that all the remaining unfulfilled prophecies will likewise be fulfilled.

Sad indeed is the fact that 1.2 billion of the world's population
stake their eternal destinies on the word of a seventh century
prophet and a book he claimed came to him from Allah. Living
700 years after the fact, he claims that Jesus Christ did not die
on the cross.

Surah 4:156 says, "That they said in boast, We
killed Christ Jesus the Son of Mary, the Messen-

ger of Allah but they killed him not, nor crucified him, but so it was made to appear to them,
and those who differ, therein are full of doubts
with no certain knowledge, but only conjecture
to follow, for a surety, they killed him not. Nay
Allah raised him up unto Himself."

There are two sets of testimonies: one from a lone man who
lived 700 years after the fact over against 500 disciples of Christ
who saw him ascend into heaven. I Corinthians 15:6. Also, the
disciples of Christ were there and saw Him die, and they saw
Him alive again. Acts 1:3 says: *"To whom also he shewed himself
alive after his passion by many infallible proofs, being seen of them
forty days, and speaking of the things pertaining to the kingdom of
God."* Put the Bible and the Koran to the two tests for truth:
correspondence to reality and coherence to logical thought. I
choose to differ with Mohammed and trust the words of honest
men who laid down their lives for the truth of the Gospel.

End Notes:

1. Zacharias, p. 43.
2. Gabriel, *Islam and the Jews,* pp. 104, 105.
3. Jones, Stanley, *The Word Made Flesh,* Abingdon Press, Nashville, TN, 1963 quoted by Anis Shorrosh in *Islam Revealed-A Christian Arab's View of Islam,* Thomas Nelson Publishers, Nashville,TN, 1988,pp. 138, 139.
4. Shorrosh, p. 139.
5. Richardson, p. 207.
6. Ibid.
7. Geisler, Norm and Saleed, Abdul, *Answering Islam—The Crescent in Light of the Cross,* Baker Books, Grand Rapids, MI, 2002, pp. 190, 191. They are quoting Al haj Ajijola, *The Essence of Faith in Islam,* Islamic Publications Ltd, Lahore, 1978, pp. 100, 101.

ROME COURTS MECCA

The papacy and Islam are a strange mix. From its beginning in the 7th century, Muslims have targeted Christendom for destruction. During its first one hundred years, it conquered all of Christian North Africa and even brought Spain into its orbit. The Roman Church under Pope Urban II initiated the Crusades in an effort to recapture the Holy Land. Islam proclaims its divine right to wage war in behalf of Allah and his prophet, but they loudly protest against anyone daring to withstand them. Some 700 years later the Ottoman Turk's great military leader, Mehmed II, finally captured Constantinople, which at that time represented the glory and power of Christendom. So historically there has been a vast gulf fixed between Islam and Christianity, and especially the Roman Catholic Church.

Islam Not So Bad After All

Since 9/11/2001 and even before, Rome has been making overtures toward Mecca. *The Wanderer (Roman Catholic Weekly)* June 3, 1999, quotes Pope John Paul II:

> The Holy Father spoke about religious dialog with Islam in his general audience on May 5th. While mentioning the point on which Christians and Muslims most differ, the mystery of the Trinity, the Pope also said that the two traditions 'have a long history of study, philosophical and theological reflection, literature and science, which have left their mark on Eastern and Western cultures,' and 'are called in one spirit of love to defend and always promote human dignity, moral values, and freedom.' Muslims together with us adore the one, merciful God. The Church has a high regard for them, convinced that their faith in the transcendent God contributed to building a new human family based on the highest aspirations of the human heart.[1]

Pope Paul II is the most widely traveled pope in history. His journeys took him to the Muslim nation of Kazakhstan, formerly of the USSR shortly after the 9/11 catastrophes. In spite of the catastrophic events of September 11th, the Pope has continued faithfully to support the Roman Catholic Church's policy of affirmation and approval of Islam. Let us listen to what he says to the people of Kazakhstan:

> 'There is one God.' The Apostle (Mohammed) proclaims before all else the absolute oneness of God. This is a truth which Christians inherited from the children of Israel and which they share with Muslims: it is faith in the one God, 'Lord of heaven and earth" (Lk. 10:21), almighty and merciful. In the name of this one God, I turn to the people of deep and ancient religious traditions, the people of Kazakhstan. This 'logic of love' is what he holds out to us, asking us to live it above all through generosity to those in need. It is a logic which can bring together Christians and Muslims, and commit them to work together for the 'civilization of love.' It is a logic that overcomes all the cunning of this world and allows us to make true friends who will welcome us 'into eternal dwelling-places' (Luke 16:9), into the 'homeland' of heaven.[2]

This Never Happened Before

Not only is the pope visiting Muslim countries, but Muslim leaders are visiting the Vatican. Iranian leader, Mohammed Khatami in August, 1999, met with Pope John Paul II for 25 minutes in the papal study. The following report was given:

> Khatami expressed to the pope that he hoped the two monotheistic faiths could join to inspire a more equitable world order in which Islamic nations are treated by the West as full partners. The hope is for the victory of monotheism, of ethics, of morals together with peace and reconciliation. Vatican officials said Khatami's visit had landmark significance for two reasons. One is Iran's influence in the Islamic world, enhanced by the fact that Khatami is now president of the 55 nation Islamic Conference. The other reason is Khatami's opening to the West after his elec-

tion 21 months ago and his effort to wrest power from hard-line conservative clerics whose policies have made Iran a pariah state.[3]

Rome Flipflops Again

In a carefully worded statement, the Roman Catholic Church officially declares that the One God of Holy Scripture is also the God of Islam. It also esteems the moral life of Islam, the affirmation of which follows:

> The Church has also a high regard for the Muslims. They worship God, who is one, living and subsistent, merciful and almighty, the Creator of heaven and earth, who has also spoken to men. They strive to submit themselves without reserve to the hidden decrees of God, just as Abraham submitted himself to God's plan, whose faith Muslims eagerly link to their own. Although not acknowledging Him as God, they venerate Jesus as a prophet, his virgin Mother they also honor, and even at times devotedly invoke. Further, they await the Day of Judgment and the reward of God following the resurrection of the dead. For this reason they highly esteem an upright life and worship God, especially by way of prayer, alms, deeds and fasting.[4]

It is clear from this official recognition that the Church of Rome's estimation of Islam has experienced a fundamental change. *The Catholic Encyclopedia's* statement of 1908 which came straight from the pope is vastly different:

> In matters political, Islam is a system of despotism at home and aggression abroad. The rights of non-Muslim subjects are of the vaguest and most limited kind, and a religious war is a sacred duty whenever there is a chance of success against the "infidel." Medieval and modern Mohammedan, especially Turkish, persecutions of both Jews and Christians are perhaps the best illustration of this fanatical religious and political spirit.[5]

What is Behind the Shift?
What is behind this novel re-assessment of the Muslim faith by the Vatican? These official statements are carefully constructed religious discourse. They are aimed at engendering a new mood of respectful rapprochement and mutual understanding between the papacy and Islam. As a device of diplomatic exchange, they show clearly that a new interfaith-ecumenicity is being propounded by Rome with the singular objective of embracing Islam and its peoples within a new international community of religious life and faith, a community incidentally, in which Rome enjoys priority as founder and senior partner.[6]

We might ask another question. Who is behind this dramatic shift in policy toward Islam? Karol Wojtyla, Pope Paul II, is the head of a totalitarian hierarchy. He is absolute monarch with his own secular government of Vatican City and more property worldwide than any other person on the planet. With his territorial dominions, cardinals, ambassadors worldwide, a detective force, legislature, jurisprudence, laws, advocates, taxes, banks, foreign treaties, ambitious plans and policies are all his. This powerful man, who is now nearing death, along with his accomplices, like Islam, has plans for world domination. With an enemy like Islam, maybe the tactic is "if you can't beat them, join them."

Evangelical Wimps
What is sad is that many evangelical leaders are cozening up to Rome the same as Rome cozies up to Islam. The publication of *Evangelicals and Catholics Together—the Third Millennium* exploded like a bombshell in 1994. Outstanding leaders both evangelical and Catholic called for a halt to proselytizing Catholics by Protestants and Protestants by Catholics.[7] With this spirit of compromise in the air, it is unlikely that these evangelical leaders will differ with Rome concerning Islam. After Franklin Graham criticized Islam as a violent, non-peaceful religion, these same leaders ran for cover like cockroaches do when exposed to light.

Bennett and Nicholson in their article on the *Papacy and Islam* foresee the following:

> In practice both of these systems, Islam and Catholicism, are totalitarian, synthesizing spiritual

and civil power in their doctrinal presentations and cultic practices. The global hierarchy and infrastructure of the RCC, however, is far more developed than that of Islam. The global bringing together of these two billion adherents under the Roman Pontiff, who calls himself the Vicar of Christ, would make for a political powerhouse of vast consequences.[7]

Where Is Islam in the Bible?

It has always been a mystery to me why Islam is not mentioned in the Bible. What is going on today between Catholicism and Islam could be the answer. The drawing of governments and religions into a global coalition is already begun. Rome has opened her gates to one and all (except Bible-believing Christians). Shamans, Hindu priests, Buddhist monks, and Muslim mullahs are all welcome and can find a home in Rome. So more than likely, Islam will be swallowed up in the Anti-Christ's one world religion. As we have seen, Islam is accepted as a valid religion by the Catholic Church, and the terrorists of September are understood to be fallen from their religion, rather than upholding its teachings. Sadly George W. Bush goes along with this deception. After 9/11 he said:

> The terrorists practice a fringe form of Islamic extremism that has been rejected by Muslim scholars and the vast majority of Muslim clerics; a fringe movement that perverts the peaceful teachings of Islam....[Islam's] teachings are good and peaceful, and those who commit evil in the name of Allah blaspheme the name of Allah ....The terrorist traitors are traitors to their own faith, trying in effect, to hijack Islam itself. These murderers have hijacked a great religion in order to justify their evil deeds. And we cannot let it stand.[8]

The Muslims themselves are giving the same message. For example the *Associated Press* reported as follows:

> An international Muslim religious ruling endorsed the morality of the U.S. led military effort against terrorists.The ruling was written by

Sheikh Yusuf al-Qaradawi, the widely respected chairman of the Sunna and Sira Council in Qatar, along with three colleagues in Egypt and one in Syria. The new fatwa cited the words of God in the Quran and authoritative Hadith....'All Muslims ought to be united against all those who terrorize the innocents, and those who permit the killing of non-combatants without a justifiable reason,' the fatwa said.[9]

This spin on Islam is perfectly in line with what the Pope and the Vatican declared: "together with us they adore the one, merciful God, mankind's judge on the last day." It looks as if the Pope, the politicians, and the Muslim clerics continue to conceal successfully the history of Mohammed and the contents of his Koran.[10]

End Notes:

1. *The Wanderer (Roman Catholic weekly)* June 3, 1999 quoted in the Christian News, Vol. 37, No 23, p. 1.

2. *Homily of the Pope in Atsana, Kazakhstan* on Sunday, September 23, 2001. http./www./vatican,va/holyfather/joh_Paulii/homilies/2001/documents/hf_jpiho_200110923_kazak.

3. Midnight Call, September, 1999, p. 41

4. Bennett, Richard and Nicholson, Robert, *New Partnership with Muslims, The Papacy and Islam,* February 2, 2002, p. 2.

5. *The Catholic Encyclopedia,* statement made in 1908.

6. Bennett and Nicholson, p. 5.

7. *"First things,"* A *Monthly Journal of Religious and Public Life,* Richard John Neuhaus, ed., Number 42, *Evangelicals and Catholics Together: The Christian Mission in the Third Millenium* (New York, May, 1994) pp. 15-22.

8. Bennett and Nicholson, p. 5.

9. Speech to Congress, 20 September 2001, quoted from Daniel Pipes, *Militant Islam Reaches America,* W.W. Norton & Company, New York, 2002, p. 96.

10. Bennett and Nicholson, p. 5.

Of course, I know that all Muslims do not hate us or the U.S.A. I also know enough about Islam, whether it be secular, moderate, or militant to know that a common, name they use for our great, generous country is "Great Satan." Let us define terms. A secular Muslim is one who does not pray, does not attend the mosque, and more than likely drinks alcohol and lives a sinful lifestyle. He is a Muslim by birth but not by faith or practice. Many secular Muslims such as Ibn Warraq, author of *Why I am Not a Muslim,* are forsaking Islam. Sadly, many of them turn to atheism. The moderate Muslim, on the other hand, holds fast to his faith and practice, but conquering the world for Islam is not his or her agenda. These people want good jobs, creature comforts, a wife, and children. If the truth were known more than likely these folks make up the majority. The militant, radical, fundamentalist Muslim whose agenda is definitely conquering the world for Islam is growing. I attended in Lawrenceville, Georgia a special lecture by Jay Smith, a missionary to Muslims in London, in which he stated that forty-five percent of Muslims in England are Osama bin Laden sympathizers. The militants are divided into three groups: "the inner core, made up of the likes of Osama bin Laden, and the nineteen hijackers;" the second group are those "who are sympathetic" with bin Laden's "vision without being a part of it;" "the third" group "consists of Muslims who do not accept the militant Islamic program in all its particulars" but are "rank anti-American." [1]

Historical Reasons

What we want to learn is why the majority of Muslims hate America and all it stands for. To understand the hatred and venom these people have toward us requires some knowledge of history and the Muslim psyche. Historically, Islam has made wrong choices. The Muslim Ottoman Empire (Turkey) in 1914 cast its lot with a loser, William Kaiser. Second, during the Second World War, Islam did not learn its lesson and supported Adolph Hitler. They loved Hitler because he hated the Jews. Finally, Islam thought that Russia and Communism were the "wave of the future" and came into the Soviet orbit. "Governments and movements" eagerly embraced various forms of socialism and fascism (Suddam Hossain) "all over the Arab world."[2] None of the above were lovers of America. The main reason, however, that the Muslims joined forces with the Nazis and the Communists were not their diverse doctrines; it was their anti-Westernism that attracted the Muslims.

Muslim Psyche

Mohammed was a winner. He only lost one battle. From 622 until 1683, Islam rolled on victoriously. Unbeknown to the Arabs and the countries they had conquered and islamized something was happening in Europe. Through the Reformers, Biblical Christianity rescued much of Europe from the clutches and corruption of Popism. As a result, England became a giant lion encircling the world with her colonies. Then her former colony, the United States, became the unchallenged leader of the world. As a result of the wrong choices mentioned above, England, France, Belgium, and the Netherlands divided the Ottoman Empire, India, Africa, and Indonesia between them. The infidels had conquered Islam.

Bob Blincoe, U.S. Director, Frontiers in his article *Honor and Shame* give insight to the Muslim mind.

> What is behind the September 11 attacks? What drives clear-minded Muslims to such extreme, calculated acts? The answer derives from two all-important values in Muslim culture: honor and shame. When these values are twisted by sin, people can become selfish, remorseless and sometimes desperate in their actions. In the Middle East, gaining and maintaining honor is more to be valued than life. Avoiding shame, and as a result, shifting the blame to others is the only response when one's honor is threatened. We had best fix this in our minds if we would understand what Muslims, even moderate Muslims, know drives some Eastern people to violence.[3]

As David Pryce-Jones says in his classic book, *The Closed Circle:*

> Honor is what makes life worthwhile; shame a living death, not to be endured, requiring that it be avenged. What otherwise seems self-destructive in Arab society is explained by anxiety to be

honored and respected at all costs, and by whatever means.[4]

To show you how this honor/shame axis controls Muslims, I quote an interview between ABC News and Osama Bin Laden in 1998.

> The call to wage war against America was made because America has spear-headed the crusade against the Islamic nation, sending tens of thousands of its troops to the land of the two Holy Mosques (Saudi Arabia). And then there is Israel. For over a half-century, Muslims in Palestine have been slaughtered and assaulted and robbed of their **honor** and of their property. They kill and murder our brothers. They compromise our **honor** and our dignity and dare we utter a single protest against the injustice, we are called terrorists.[5] *(author's emphasis)*

Bob Blincoe, U.S. Director, frontiers from the following statement evidences that he knows the Muslim mind quite well.

> Bin Laden says that America compromised Muslim honor. This is the point Bin Ladin wants to make, and we had better hear him if we're to understand him and many other extreme Muslims. Honor is more to be sought, and disgrace more to be avoided, than all the jewels in a king's crown. If there were no Israel and no America, the honor/shame axis would still control the thoughts and actions of Easterners, just as gaining wealth control thoughts and actions of people in the West.[6]

So America, now the Great Satan, has become the scapegoat for Islam.

America the Tempter

Muslims have a bad opinion of Americans. Most of the *dhimmis,* Christians who paid the tax and remained Christians in Muslim lands, were of the Eastern Orthodox or Roman Catholic faith or some other heretical sect. Their manner of life did not impress the Muslims. In the Muslim country in which I lived for seventeen years, the Muslims associated Christianity with a dissolute life of immorality and alcohol. They were sincerely shocked to see the testimony of born again Christians who loved God with all their hearts and lived cleaner lives than the Muslims. It was joy not only to preach the gospel to Muslims, but also to live the gospel before them.

Sayyid Qutb, an Egyptian official in the Ministry of Education, was sent on a special study mission to the United States in 1948. He later was jailed in Egypt for terrorism. In 1964, he released one of his major works, *Signposts On The Way,* which was a best seller in the Arab world. His perverted idea of America is recorded in his book. Historian Bernard Lewis records Qutb's impressions of America:

> He was shocked principally by its (America's) sinfulness and degeneracy and its addiction to what he saw as sexual promiscuity.... Everything in America, he wrote, even religion, is measured in material terms. He observed that there were many churches but warned his readers that their numbers should not be misunderstood as an expression of real religious or spiritual feeling. Churches in America, he said, operate like businesses, competing for clients and for publicity, and using the same methods as stores and theaters to attract customers and audiences....To attract clientele, churches advertise shamelessly and offer what most Americans most seek—'a good time' or 'fun.' The result is that church recreation halls, with the blessing of the priesthood, hold dances where people of both sexes meet, mix, and touch. The ministers go so far as to dim the lights in order to facilitate the fury of the dance, he noted with evident disgust; 'the dance area is inflamed by the notes of the gramophone', the dance-hall becomes a whirl of heels and thighs, arms enfold hips, lips and breasts meet, and the air is full of lust.[7]

Consider what America exports to the Muslim world: rock music, Levi jeans, Hollywood movies, and ungodly TV programs. It is no wonder Muslims think America is a cesspool of iniquity. Ayatolla Khomeini coined the term "Great Satan" for America. Satan as depicted in the Qu'ran is neither an imperialist nor an exploiter. He is a seducer, "the insidious tempter who whispers in the hearts of men" Surah 114:4,5 "Who whispers into the hearts of men, From among the jinn and the men.[8]

America's Military Prowess

Since the rise of Islam, history records a continual conflict with Christendom. So it is no surprise that Muslims fear American power. Muslims view the West as Christian, and during the colonial period (1450–1970), they felt the wrath of military power. "Spain and Portugal led the way.... with their warrior-missionary adventures. The next century saw the Dutch, French, and English enter the field in a mad race to build empires. Before it was over, Belgium, Germany, Italy, and Russia had jumped into the game." Even though these countries were not operating as Christian in any sense of the word, the Muslims do not acknowledge that fact. At one time, ninety-percent of Islamic countries were under colonial domination. The wounds inflicted on Islam are still fresh in Muslim minds and hearts.[9]

America also has been very active militarily in the Muslim world. She invaded Lebanon in 1956; forced France, Britain and Israel to back off from seizing the Suez Canal in 1956; went to war with Iraq to expel its forces from Kuwait; and more recently defeated the Taliban in Afghanistan and Saddam Hussein in Iraq. So in their eyes the Muslims have every right to fear and hate America.[10]

Support of Israel

In the matter of relations between Islam and America, the straw that "broke the camel's back" is our defense of Israel. "America was the first country to recognize the state of Israel following the United Nations Resolution of 1948. Ever since then, in the eyes of Muslims, Americans have been perceived as the power behind Israel, and hence the real enemy of Islam. Muslims ever since the Jewish victory in the War of 1967 feel they have been deprived of one of their most treasured possessions: Jerusalem." Pilgrims seek to worship at the Dome of the Rock and al-Aska Mosque, both in Jerusalem.... from all over the Muslim world. In addition, the Muslims have not forgotten that the Jews drove Palestinians out of their land in 1948, and forced them to leave their farms, orchards, businesses and homes. Still today they languish in refugee camps.[11]

The explosion of outrage in the Muslim world was instantaneous. The Muslims have never forgotten. Every ruler of Saudi Arabia from the late King Faisal to the present has proclaimed a jihad (holy war) against Israel. Moral and financial support given to Israel by both the U.S. government and the Christian churches makes the U.S.A. and the Christian Church the ultimate enemy of Islam.[12]

End Notes:

1. Pipes, Daniel, *Militant Islam Reaches America,* W.W. Norton and company, New York, 2003, pp. 246, 247.
2. Lewis, p. 71.
3. Blincoe,Bob, *Honor and Shame, An Open Letter to Evangelical Leaders,* Missions Frontiers, December, 2001, p. 19.
4. Pryce-Jones, David, *The Closed Circle,* p. 35.
5. Blincoe quoting an ABC Interview with Osama bin Laden, p. 19.
6. Ibid.
7. Lewis, p. 78, 79.
8. Ibid., p. 86
9. McCurry, Don, *Islam and Christian Militarism,* Mission Frontiers, December, 2002, pp. 24-26.
10. Ibid.
11. Ibid.
12. Ibid.

BLAME GAME
CHAPTER FOURTEEN

A careful observer will have noticed that Islamic organizations are becoming increasingly bold in challenging anyone who dares to speak out against Islam. Whether one is speaking the truth is not relevant to them. If the information in any wise casts a bad light on Islam, then they will go after the source with unrelenting zeal. Our intent in this chapter is to give examples of this brazen contempt for the first amendment by these Islamists. Sad to say, the media, the liberals, and our government seem to be on their side.

Plague on the Postal Service

The power of the Islamic lobby in our government continues to grow. Jack Moody of Lenoir, NC went to the U.S. Post Office to send his son, Daniel, a serviceman in Iraq, a care package containing a Bible Study and other Christian material for his edification. The Postmaster told him that due to USPS, Postal Bulletin 22097, Section E1, he could not send any matter containing religious material contrary to the Islamic faith, any nude or semi-nude photos, or any pornographic material. It might offend some Muslim overseas. Jack Moody made a statement to the news media to this effect: "My son is in the military, and he is fighting to free this country from tyranny and to protect our rights and freedom. Our government has a rule that limits that freedom. I just couldn't believe it."[1] This inane rule was initiated during the Gulf War by the work of zealous Islamists coupled with uninformed Postal officials. Things like this make my red American blood boil.

Church Sign in Florida

Rev. Gene Youngblood teaches a World Religion course at Conservative Theological Seminary in Jacksonville, FL. In January, 2003 Rev. Youngblood used his knowledge of the Koran on his church billboard. It read like this: Jesus forbad murder— Matthew 26:52. Muhammad approved murder - Surah 8:65 says, "O Prophet! urge the believers to war; if there are twenty patient ones of you they shall overcome two hundred, and if there are a hundred of you they shall overcome a thousand of those who disbelieve, because they are a people who do not understand."

Bob Jones in *World* magazine described the incident as follows:

> A local imam (leader of the mosque) argued that the passage referred not to murder but to standing fast on the battlefield. The Council on American Islamic Relations (CAIR) news release accused the Florida pastor of misinformation and called on Floridians to repudiate Mr. Youngblood. "All Americans must band together to condemn hate speech designed to divide our nation along ethnic lines. Any attempt to marginalize or vilify one religious community is an attack on all people of faith."[2]

I personally think he made a poor choice of surahs in making his case. Mr. Youngblood reports that "we've had threats. We've had viciousness. We've had violence. The sign has been vandalized more than a dozen times until it was put under 24-hour surveillance."[3]

Freedom of Speech

Islamic organizations sponsored Senate Resolution 133, an innocent-appearing motion titled 'Supporting religious tolerance toward Muslims.' Its content, though, is not so innocent. It reads as follows:

> Muslims have been subjected, simply because of their faith, to acts of discrimination and harassment that all too often have led to hate-inspired violence and concludes that **any criticism of Islam,** though legal, is morally reprehensible: while the Senate respects and upholds the right of individuals to free speech, the Senate acknowledges that individuals and organizations that foster such intolerance create an atmosphere of hatred and fear that divides the Nation.[4] *(author's emphasis)*

How clever these Islamists are! Any mention of Muslims or Islam that is not favorable is construed by them as discrimination and harassment.

Shutting Down the Debate
Daniel Pipes describes the tactics of intimidation as follows:

> Khomeini used blunt methods to shut down debate in Iran. Since the Islamists in America cannot use blunt methods in our society yet, they do so by conducting hostile campaigns against anyone who runs afoul of their views.... While their efforts generally do not include overt threats of violence, they tend to be exceedingly unpleasant, with the effect that only the most determined individuals decide to address these topics. Taken in the context of the worldwide use of violence against critics, militant Islamic efforts in the United States have an unmistakable stench of intimidation about them.[5]

The Council on American Islamic Relations (CAIR) is one of the more aggressive intimidators. It fronts as a civil rights organization protecting Muslims from harassment. Its main agenda is helping Hamas against Israel and promoting militant Islam's agenda in the United States. Steve Pomerantz, a former chief of counterterrorism for the FBI, explains that "any objective assessment... leads to the conclusion that CAIR, its leaders, and its activities, effectively give aid to international terrorists groups. Unfortunately, CAIR is but one of a new generation of new groups in the United States that hide under a veneer of 'civil rights' or 'academic' status but in fact are tethered to a platform that supports terrorism."[6]

When CAIR sends out one of its "action alerts," dozens and even hundreds of protests, many of them vulgar and aggressive, is the result.

Taking on the Big Boys
Daniel Pipes in his hard-hitting book, *The Militants Among Us,* has done all of us a service by exposing the intimidators. Here are a few examples. CAIR is not afraid to take on the "Big Boys." They picketed the *Dallas Morning News* for revealing the Hamas infrastructure in Texas.[7] Muslims launched a campaign against the *Tampa Tribune* for uncovering the Islamic Jihad in Tampa.[8] And what is one to make of its attempt to censor a magazine for children, *The Weekly Reader,* on account of its

December 2, 1996, issue carrying an anodyne (comforting) article on terrorism, even though it almost entirely avoids mentioning Islam?[9] CAIR also denounced the *Atlantic Monthly* for an article on militant Islamic violence in Sudan and a Senate Subcommittee for holding hearings on Foreign Terrorists in America: Five Years After the World Trade Center Bombing.[10]

Silencing Critics

As CAIR promotes militant Islam in the United States, it focuses on one main point: silencing those who have anything negative to say about militant Islam. It attacked the Wiesenthal Center for portraying Ayatollah Khomeini as a Hitler-like enemy of the Jews.[11] Likewise, it went after *Reader's Digest* for documenting the repression of Christians in several Muslim countries.[12] Father Richard Neuhaus, editor of *First Things,* wrote in October 1997 a negative review of historical Islam:

> Islam's spectacular spread was brought about by brutal military conquest, rapine, spoliation, and slavery. 'Islamic civilization' was derived from the vanquished. The Islamic world stews in its resentments and suspicions, alternating with low-grade jihad in the form of the persecution of Christians, international terrorism, and dreams of driving Israel into the sea. The biggest problem in sight is Islam.[13]

In response CAIR called on the Catholic Church "to investigate Neuhaus" and its followers sent him cascades of abusive mail accusing him of being "obviously mentally ill" and "doing the work of Adolph Hitler."[14]

Faithful General Under Attack

Lt. Gen William Boykin, a much decorated soldier, was wounded by the political correctness movement. He is being maligned for comparing the war against militant Islam to a battle against Satan. General Boykin, who is Deputy Undersecretary of Defense, has told Christian audiences that radical Islam threatens to destroy America "because we're a Christian nation." In muzzling Gen. Boykin, the Pentagon has not converted those who believe they have a religious mandate to destroy us. It is silencing, instead of sounding, the alarm that this enemy is bigger than any threat America has ever faced. [15]

When Lies Are Justified

Philosopher Ibn Taymiyah (1263-1328) wrote a book titled *The Sword on the Neck of the Accuser of Muhammad.* In it he described how Muslims should live when they are in the minority:

> Believers when in a weakened stage in a non-Muslim country should forgive and be patient with People of the Book [i.e., Jews and Christians] when they insult Allah and his prophet by any means. Believers should lie to People of the Book to protect their lives and religion.[16]

"In other words it's OK to lie to non-Muslims to protect yourself when you are a minority in their country. There's an Islamic proverb that says 'if you can't cut your enemies' hand, kiss it.'"[17] When Mohammed was weak in Mecca, he was a lamb. When he was strong in Medina, he was a lion. Muslims living in predominantly Muslim countries do not hesitate to oppress and persecute Christians and Jews. "On the other hand, Muslims living in Christian nations or nations where the majority profess to be Christians are very good at presenting themselves as loving, caring and forgiving people." Muslims in minority status call Christians and Jews brothers and present Islam to these countries as the answer to all humanity's problems. "Westernized Muslims present their religion as if it stands for mercy, freedom, fairness and reconciliation. They portray Islam as a religion that does not show any prejudice to any race or culture."[18]

Mosque: For Worship or For War

"During the U.S. bombing campaign in Afghanistan, the U.S. military bombed a mosque on October 23, 2001. The Lebanese News Center complained, 'People who were praying inside were killed and injured.'"[19] "Most of the Muslims interviewed by Western media present Islam as a religion only and that the mosque is just like a church or synagogue, a place of worship. However, the mosque during the prophet Mohammed's time was not just a place of worship. It was a place to store weapons and make military plans. In Medina, Mohammed used the mosque there as the headquarters for all his wars."[20]

The same is happening in America. The FBI infiltrated a Jersey City mosque in which Sheikh Omar Abdul Rahman, a 57-year-old blind Egyptian Muslim cleric, who was involved in the attempted assassination of Hosni Mubarak, was presiding. He continually denounced the United States and Israel and called for a "holy jihad" against America. The informer with a hidden video camera and tape recorder recorded the group as they made plans for the Day of Terror. The plan involved simultaneous strikes at the United Nations headquarters, the Lincoln and Holland tunnels, the George Washington Bridge, and the Federal Office at 26 Federal Plaza. Thankfully, their evil plans were thwarted and all nine defendants were found guilty and jailed.[21]

Unsung American Patriot

Steve Emerson was a reporter with CNN and inadvertently attended a meeting in a mosque where anti-American rhetoric and calls for jihad piqued his curiosity. This began a long investigative research that led to the production of *"Jihad in America"* video. It was broadcast on PBS November 21, 1994 at 10 p.m. CAIR attacked the content and the producer and did their best to deny what was really going on. Despite all of the attacks, the video won the "prestigious George Polk Award" and "was also named the best investigative reporting in print, broadcast or book by the Investigative Reporters and Editors Organization."[22] To show you how Muslims deal with people who dare expose them, note what happened:

> Death threats began to come... I got an urgent call from U.S. law enforcement officials. I was working in my Washington apartment. They told me to get in a taxi and come downtown immediately, making sure no one was following me... When I got there, it turned out to be the offices of the Bureau of Diplomatic Security (BDS), an arm of the state department that deals largely with terrorism.
> FBI and BDS officials quickly briefed me. After *"Jihad in America"* aired in South Africa, a militant Muslim group had taken offense. They had dispatched a team to assassinate me... As far as they knew the assassins had already entered the country and probably had me under surveillance.[23]

Steve Emerson had several choices: keep quiet and don't write about militant Islam anymore; get in a federal witness protection program by moving to another city and assuming another identity; or stay in a safe house for a year. He chose none of the above options but continues to this day gathering data on militant Islam. You can read his research in his book, *American Jihad—The Terrorists Living Among Us.* He cautiously yet bravely goes about his work. He is surely a great American patriot.

End Notes:

1. Pyle, Norman *Christian View of the News,* October 2003.
2. Jones, Bob, *World Magazine,* March 22, 2003, pp. 17, 18.
3. Ibid.
4. Pipes, pp. 175, 176.
5. Ibid.
6. *Counterterrorism in a Free Society, Journal of Countertewrrorism & Security International,* Spring, 1998.
7. *The New York Times,* article on Muslims picketing the *Dallas News,* February 11, 1996.
8. Council on American-Islamic Relations, *The Tampa Tribune* and Steve Emerson, 15 April Florida.
9. CAIR, *Educational Publication Says Muslims Set Pattern for Terrorism,* 15 September 1996 criticizing *The Weekly Reader* for an article designed to comfort children frightened by terrorism.
10. Letters to the Editor, *The Atlantic Monthly,* September 1994; CAIR, Senate Hearing on Foreign Terrorists in America, 20 January 1998.
11. CAIR, *Americans Muslims Say Museum Associated with Wiesenthal Center Promotes Intolerance toward Islam,* 3 December 1997.
12. CAIR. " *'Global War on Christians' Smears Islam: Muslims Asked to Challenge One-Sided Reader's Digest* Article," 24, July 1997.
13. CAIR, *First Things Journal Editor Defames Islam,* 16 October 1997.
14. Neuhaus, Richard, I*slamic Encounters, First Things,* February 1998.
15. Thomas, Cal, *World Magazine,* November 1, 2003, p. 9.
16. Ibn Taymiyah, Al-Sarim Almslowl Allah Shatem Alrasool, *The Sword on the Neck of the Accuser of Muhammad,* p. 21.
17. Gabriel, p. 92.
18. Ibid.
19. Source obtained from the Internet: *"U.S. bombs hit Mosque, Kills 15 worshippers,"* Lebanon News Center at www.lebanon-guide.com (October 24, 2001.
20. Gabriel, pp. 97,98.
21. Branigin, William and Chandrasekaran, Rajiv, *"Informants Enable a Deadly Raid,"* Washington Post (October 25, 2001), p. A10.
22. Emerson, Steve, *American Jihad—The Terrorist Living Among Us,* The Free Press, New York, 2002, pp. 13. 14
23. Ibid., p. 15.

Without controversy, Islam is a great religion with a profound tradition. Many positives can be found in Islam: a tenacious faith in Allah and his prophet Mohammed; an unyielding loyalty and obedience to the Koran; a strong emphasis on the family; a stand against the moral evils of our day, i.e., abortion, homosexuality, pornography, alcohol, and drugs. Islamic scholars over the centuries have labored to develop an intricate legal system. Muslims rally to Islam and are quick to defend their brothers when they are attacked. Having said all that, I intend in this chapter to show from history and from the Koran what is the ultimate aim of Islam.

Islam's Decline

Islam at one time controlled the world, and during that time (750-1300), great advances occurred in literature, architecture, science, astronomy, mathematics, medicine, sociology, and banking. However, there came a time when Islam began to atrophy while at the same time Christendom awoke and began to advance. Muslim society has a hard time explaining their loss of prominence and power.

> Individual Muslims have flourished, but their societies and countries have remained well behind the West. Whatever index one looks at, Muslims can be found clustering toward the bottom, whether in terms of military prowess, political stability, economic development, corruption, lack of human rights, health, longevity, or literacy. Anwar Ibrahim, the former deputy prime minister of Malaysia, estimates that whereas Muslims make up just one fifth of the world's total population, they constitute more than half of the 1.2 billion people living in abject poverty... There is a pervasive sense of debilitation, encroachment, and things having gone seriously wrong. As a Muslim religious leader in Jerusalem put it, "Before, we were masters of the world and now we're not even masters of our own mosques."[1]

Traditional Versus Militant Islam

Daniel Pipes, Harvard scholar and Islamic specialist, author of *Militant Islam Reaches America,* is a brave and honest writer. But I challenge his premise that there is a great chasm between traditional Islam and militant Islam. According to Pipes, "traditional Islam seeks to teach human beings how to live in accord with God's will; militant Islam aspires to create a new order."[2] He poses the question "does Islam threaten the West?" He answers, "no it does not." "But militant Islam does threaten it in many and profound ways."[3] I would remind Mr. Pipes that the traditionalist and the militant read from the same Koran. There is not a Muslim worth his salt that will dare argue against the Koran or the Hadith. Maybe Mr. Pipes is trying to win points by contrasting so drastically traditional and militant Islam.

Where Are the Traditionalists?

Since 9/11 Muslims have come under suspicion which can be expected since all 19 hijackers were Muslims. Everyone knows that all Muslims are not violent nor do they desire to overthrow our government. Serge Trifkovic says it well: "Moderate [Muslims] are not rare, but they are rarely important. Religions, like political ideologies, are pushed along by money, power, and tiny vocal minorities."[4] However, Islamic organizations that represent the rank and file Muslims in the U.S. have not distanced themselves from the militant Muslims calling for "holy jihad." Few have been the voices questioning the rightness of the attacks on the World Trade Center and the Pentagon. Islamic scholar and devout Muslim, Muqtedar Khan, director of International Studies and the Center of the Study of Islam and Democracy at Adrian College, Michigan has dared to speak out:

> What happened on September 11th in New York and Washington, DC will forever remain a horrible scar on the history of Islam and humanity. No matter how much we condemn it, and point to the Quran and the Sunnah to argue that Islam forbids the killing of innocent people, the fact remains the perpetrators of this crime against humanity have indicated that their actions are sanctioned by Islamic values. The fact that even now several Muslim scholars and thousands of Muslims defend the accused is indicative that not all Muslims believe that the attacks are un-

Islamic. This is truly sad... Muslims love to live
in the US but also love to hate it. Many openly
claim that the US is a terrorist state but they continue to live in it. Their decision to live here is
testimony that they would rather live here than
anywhere else. As an Indian Muslim, I know for
sure that nowhere else on earth, including India, will I get the same sense of dignity and respect that I have received in the US. No Muslim
country will treat me as well as the US has. If
what happened on September 11th had happened in India, the biggest democracy, thousands
of Muslims would have been slaughtered in ri-
ots on mere suspicion and there would be another slaughter after confirmation... But [here]
hundreds of Americans gathered around Islamic
centers in symbolic gestures of protection... It is
time for soul searching... How can Islam inspire
thousands of youths to dedicate their lives to killing others? We are supposed to invite people to
Islam not murder them. The worst exhibition of
Islam has happened on our turf. We must take
first responsibility to undo the evil it has manifest. This is our mandate, our burden and also
our opportunity.[5]

These are good words. They are not the words of a true Muslim but the words of a Muslim who has been profoundly touched
by a Christian worldview.

Three Stages of Jihad

Mark Gabriel, an Islamic scholar with a PH. D. in Islamic
history from Al-Azhar University in Cairo, Egypt, explains the
three stages of jihad from the Koran. First, there is the **weakened** stage. This stage applies to Muslims living as a minority
in a non-Muslim country. "At this stage, Muslims follow the
word given to Mohammed in Mecca: There is no compulsion in
religion" (Surah 2:256, *The Noble Koran*).[6] The media quotes
this verse to prove that Islam does not compel or force anyone
to convert. Remember that the verses that speak of no compulsion and "living quietly with unbelievers" were received by
Mohammed when his group was weak and threatened. "After
his movement gained strength, Mohammed received new words
that canceled out (*nasikh*) these verses.[7]

The **preparation** stage is reached "when the Muslims are a reasonably influential minority. Because their future goal is direct confrontation with the enemy, they make preparations in every possible area—financial, physical, military, mental and any other area."[8]

> Surah 8:59-60 says, Let not the Unbelievers think that they can get the better (of the godly): they will never frustrate (them). *Against them make ready your strength to the utmost of your power,* including steeds of war, to strike terror into (the hearts) of the enemies, of Allah and your enemies, and others besides whom you may not know, but whom Allah knows. (*Emphasis added.*)[9]

Modern commentary in the translation, *The Noble Koran,* says "And make ready against them all you can of power, including steeds of war (tanks, planes, missiles, artillery) to threaten the enemy of Allah "confirms to the reader that Muslims are practicing this verse for modern times (*Emphasis added.*)"[10]

The **jihad** stage commences "when Muslims are a minority with strength, influence and power. At this stage every Muslim's duty is to actively fight the enemy, overturning the system of the non-Muslim country and establishing Islamic authority. This stage is based on the final revelation [Mohammed] received concerning jihad, which is Surah 9:5. "Fight and slay the Pagans wherever you find them, and seize them, beleaguer them, and lie in wait for them in every stratagem (of war). Muslims are commanded to kill everyone who chooses not to convert to Islam. The verse says Wherever you find them. There are no geographical limits."[11] This is Koranic Islam. Call it what you may, traditional, moderate, radical, militant, fundamentalist Islam, but you may rest assured that all true Muslims believe and obey their book.

Illustration from Ancient History

"These three stages are exactly what the prophet Mohammed lived out." During the first stage while in Mecca, "he showed no animosity toward his enemies" as he was trying to win them by persuasion. After being welcomed in Medina, "he spent his first year preparing his army (Phase 2)." When he had developed sufficient strength, he declared jihad, went back to fight his enemies, completely conquered Mecca and brought it under his authority.[12] Since Mohammed is the Muslim ideal, why should we think it strange that today they are using the same strategy?

Illustration from Modern History

The county of Lebanon provides us with a current example of the three stages of taking a country for Islam. During stage 1, the Muslims cooperated with the Christian majority. They lived in peace and harmony with no talk about jihad or holy war when they were weak. "Slowly but surely, in the 1970's the preparation stage began as the Muslims received help from Libya and Iran. In the 3rd stage the Muslims began a long, destructive civil war which ravaged one of the most beautiful countries in the world. After twenty years of struggle, the Muslims could not claim victory. "Right now Lebanon has a secular government with a Christian president and a Muslim Prime Minister." They are presently back to stage 1, but when able the cycle will start again.[13]

Islamizing of America

The goal of islamizing America is not new. In the 1920's the first Islamic missionaries from abroad unblushingly stated their aim. "Our plan is, we are going to conquer America." Their claim did not go unnoticed, as a 1922 newspaper commentary shows:

> To the millions of American Christians who have so long looked eagerly forward to the time the cross shall be supreme in every land and the people of the whole world shall have become the followers of Christ, the [Muslim] plan to win this continent to the paths of the "infidel Turk" will seem a thing unbelievable. But there is no doubt about its being pressed with all the fanatical zeal for which the Mohammedans are noted.[14]

While serving in a Muslim country forty years ago, a Muslim cleric stated to me emphatically that they would "islamize" America. At the time, it seemed ludicrous but not anymore. Listen to the voices calling for an Islamic America. Ismail Al-Faruqi, a Palestinian immigrant and professor at Temple University said, "Nothing could be greater than this youthful, vigorous, and rich continent [North America] turning away from its past evil and marching under the banner of Allahu Akbar

[God is great]."[15] Zaid Shakir, formerly the Muslim chaplain at Yale University says, "Muslims cannot accept the legitimacy of the secular system in the United States, for it is against the orders and ordainments of Allah... the orientation of the Qu'ran pushes us in the exact opposite direction as the forces that are at work in the American political spectrum."[16] Ahmed Nawful, a leader of the Jordanian Muslim Brethren, denigrates the United States like this: "The United States has no doctrine and no ideology, no thought, no values and no ideals... and if Islamists stand up, with the ideology that we possess, it will be very easy for us to preside over this world again."[17]

Shamim Siddiqi has written a 168-page book with a fancy Arabic title which can be translated *The Need to Convert Americans to Islam*. In it he lays out a detailed justification and plan for Islamists to take over the United States. Look at a few of his comments:

> The future of the Muslim world now depends on how soon the Muslims of America are able to build up their own indigenous movement. Establishing militant Islam in America would signal the triumph of this ideology over its only rival, the bundle of Christianity and liberalism that constitutes Western civilization. Joining Islam and the United States makes for an ideal team. The United States is more successful than any country with a Muslim majority, but it lacks a guiding ideology and is decaying morally. Bringing together this successful country with that superb ideology makes for an extraordinary combination. The establishment of God's Kingdom on earth is no longer "a distant dream..." To achieve it, all Muslims must devote all their energies, talents and resources in building and strengthening the Islamic Movement in America.[18]

Two Ways of Conquering America

From the above, there is no doubt America is in the sights of Islamists. But how to accomplish this feat causes controversy. Will it be revolution or will it be evolution? First, let us discuss revolution. The two heroes of militant Islamists that would overthrow the United States by violence are Osama bin Laden and the blind sheik, Omar Abdel Rahman. He calls on Muslims to "conquer the land of the infidels."[19] The purpose of bombing the World Trade Center in 1993 according to his followers was to "bring down their highest buildings and the mighty constructions they are so proud of, in order thoroughly to demoralize them."[20]

The events of 9/11 did not demoralize our country. It put iron in our wills teaching the Islamists that America is no paper tiger. Their nefarious attacks united Americans as nothing has done since Pearl Harbor. Omar is in prison and Osama is running for his life.

Terrorists attacks on America put the heat on Muslim Americans. This violent anti-Americanism turns off some American Muslim converts. Jeffrey Lang, an American who converted to Islam, was amazed at what he heard while attending a mosque in San Francisco not long after his conversion. He reports the following words of an immigrant medical student:

> We must never forget—and this is extremely important—that as Muslims, we are obligated to desire, and when possible to participate in, the overthrow of any non-Muslim government—anywhere in the world—in order to replace it with an Islamic one.

Lang protested to the lecturer that if what he said was true then accepting Islam was tantamount to an act of political treason. "Yes, that's true the lecturer blithely replied."[21] The recent convert was appalled.

The nonviolent approach, evolution, has a brighter future. Going about to establish a strong Muslim presence is perfectly legal in our set up. This method does not alienate loyal Americans; it presumably works with Americans and not against them. Most Islamists have adopted this approach and seek to present Islam as very beneficial to our society. A teacher at an Islamic School in Jersey City, NJ explains their aims: "Our short-term goal is to introduce Islam. In the long term, we must save American society."[22]

There are three possible means of increasing the Muslim presence in American society: immigration, reproduction, and conversion. Since there could be a backlash if Muslim immigrants overwhelm this county, it is more likely that the main emphasis will be reproduction and conversion. Be assured that most

Muslim families do not practice birth control. To them, the more the better. Sounding like a Baptist evangelist, Shamim Siddiqi has this to say:

> American Muslims have no choice in the matter—they are "ordained by Allah" to do it [win converts to Islam]. Muslims in the United States "have no right to breathe" unless they replace evil with good. Wherever you came from, you came to America. And you came for one reason—for one reason only—to establish Allah's din [faith], as a servant of Allah.[23]

The $64 thousand question is will they succeed? In the next chapter, we will notice some unlikely cheerleaders for Islam.

End Notes:

1. Pipes, pp. 5, 6.
2. Ibid., p. 10.
3. Pipes, p. 1.
4. Trifkovic, p. 400.
5. Muqtedar Khan, M.A, *A Memo to American Muslims,* Ijtihad, pp. 1-6.
6. Gabriel, p. 86.
7. Ibid.
8. Ibid.
9. Ibid., p. 87
10. Ibid.
11. Ibid.
12. Ibid., p. 88.
13. Ibid., p. 89.
14. *Syracuse Sunday Herald,* 25 June 1922. Quoted in Richard Brent Turner, *Islam in the African-American Experience,* Indiana University Press. Bloomington, 1997, p. 122.
15. Al-Faruqi, Ismail, *Islamic Ideals in North America,* Earle Waugh, Baha Abu-Laban, and Regula B. Qureshi, eds., The Muslim Community in North America, Edmonton, Canada, University of Alberta Press, 1983, p. 269.
16. *The Role of Muslims in the Political Process,* videotape distributed by the International Institute of Islamic Research, Burlington, NJ, 1992
17. Lecture in Arabic at a MAYA convention in Kansas City in 1989.
18. Siddqi, Shamim, *Methodology of Dawah Ilallah in American Perspective, The forum for Islamic Work,* Brooklyn, NY, 1989. p. 69.
19. Detroit, 1991, Quoted in PBS documentary, *Jihad in America,* 21 November 1994.
20. Words found in a notebook kept by El-Sayyid Nossair, the Egyptian immigrant who assassinated Rabbi Meir Kahane in a New York hotel in November, 1990.
21. Jeffrey Lang, *Even Angels Ask, A Journey to Islam in America,* Amana, Beltville, Md, 1997, p. 117.
22. Frooq, Mohammed O., *Muslim American Dream, the Minaret,* Los Angeles, 1995.
23. Siddiqi, p. 76.

New words are constantly being added to our vocabulary and to our dictionaries. Two of these words are Islamophobia and Islamophilia. It seems that in America today it is popular to be an Islamophile, i.e., someone who loves and appreciates Islam. To be an Islamophobe, i.e., someone who is afraid of Islam, is equal to being a bigot, an obscurantist, or worse.

Islam's big cheerleader is none other than Bill Clinton. Addressing the General Assembly of the United Nations, he ridiculed those who "say there is an inevitable clash between Western civilization and Western values, and Islamic civilization and values" and called Islam "as American as apple pie":

> I believe this wrong. False prophets may use and abuse any religion to justify whatever political objectives they have—even cold blooded murder. Some may have the world to believe that almighty God himself, the merciful, grants a license to kill. But this is not our understanding of Islam... There are over 1200 mosques and Islamic centers in the United States, and the number is rapidly increasing. The six million Americans who worship there will tell you there is no inherent clash between Islam and America. Americans respect and honor Islam.[1]

Mr. Clinton obviously is not reading, listening, and observing the fact that tolerance and loyalty to our republic is not typical of many American Muslims. His defense of Islam as a peaceful religion does not display his magnanimity but his ignorance of what Muslims say, do, and believe, and have done for thirteen centuries.

Unholy Alliance: Islam and Liberalism

First, it was communism. The liberals and academia were enthralled with its idealistic goals of everyone sharing alike: an egalitarian utopia. Their intense hatred of the Christian faith caused them to choose bedfellows of any who may have the possibility of destroying it. This truth is too evident to be overlooked or denied. "While any attempt to bring the Bible or traditional teachings Thanksgiving, Christmas, Easter, etc., into our "public" (government) "schools" brings forth "howls of protest" of "separation of church (religion) and state." A teacher was discharged from her job for wearing a cross about her neck. Thankfully, sanity ruled and she was reinstated. "The Kuran is now required reading in one California school district as part of course work introducing students to Islam. The course requires seventh-graders not only to learn the tenets of Islam and study the important figures of the faith, but also to wear a robe, adopt a Muslim name, memorize Kuranic verses, to pray 'in the name of Allah, the Compassionate, the Merciful' and to chant, "Praise to Allah Lord of Creation." [2]

An outraged teacher, Elizabeth Christina Lemmings, expressed her outrage as follows:

> We can't even mention the name of Jesus in the public schools, but they teach Islam as the true religion, and students are taught about Islam and how to pray to Allah. Can you imagine the barrage of lawsuits and problems we would have from the ACLU if Christianity were taught in the public schools, and if we tried to teach about the contributions of Matthew, Mark, Luke, John and the Apostle Paul? But when it comes to furthering the Islamic religion in the public schools there is not one word from the ACLU, People for the American Way, or anybody else. This is hypocrisy.[3]

This California example is living proof that liberals in education are making an alliance with Islam. Since Marx failed them in destroying our Western civilization and its traditional faith in Christ and the Bible, Islam offers a helping hand to those who want to subvert the traditions of the West.

Naiveté of Mainstream Conservatives

President George W. Bush with his fervor to fight terrorism is not taking notice of the potential threat living safely and legally within our borders. In his remarks after 9/11 he stated that "Muslims make an incredibly valuable contribution to our country" and went on in his inimitable style to talk about "mom and dads who pay their bills on time." Linda Frum made this observation: "But those same mild-mannered moms and dads who pay their bills on time sometimes end up becoming terrorists, because wherever there is Islamic extremism there's a nexus to the potential of violence... Anybody who subscribes to the tenets of militant Islamic fundamentalism is capable of violence."[4]

America welcomes immigrants from all over the world. Most of these immigrants now consider themselves Americans and try to fit in with the scheme of things. Note the words of Serge Trifkovic, a journalist and learned scholar:

> The Muslim population within North America, and the rest of the West is not like any other, for it is the only immigrant group that harbors a substantial segment of individuals who share the key objectives with the terrorists, even if they do not all approve of their methods. It would be idle for even ardent Islamic apologists to pretend that many Muslim immigrants do not despise the West in general and the United States in particular, its institutions and all it stands for. To them their host country is a **mine to be stripped, used and converted or destroyed.** This was not what other newcomers to America had in mind as they flocked here to enjoy the unique opportunities of freedom. It was not what the African Americans fought for as they justly demanded their rights under the Constitution during the civil rights movement. As is evident in the actions and words of many American Muslims a sizable minority of them wishes to transform their host country into a Muslim country— by whatever means, violent or otherwise, justified by the supposed sanctity of the goal and a corresponding Koranic injunction. *(Author's emphasis)*[5]

America's Big Mistake

American foreign policy as it relates to Islamic countries has been a fiasco. Our purpose is to show the problems we now face in Iraq, Iran, Afghanistan, Saudi Arabia, and Palestine all are the result of failed foreign policy. There is a saying that "what goes around comes around." The failed strategy to which I refer is in supporting Islamic ambitions in pursuit of short-term political or military objectives which has helped turn Islamic radicalism into a truly global phenomenon.[6] Osama bin Laden and his Al Quaida network were funded by hundreds of millions of dollars and trained to fight the Russians in Afghanistan. When former National Security Advisor Zbigniew Brzezinski was asked if he regretted having supported Islamic fundamentalism, giving arms and advice to future terrorists he answered: "What matters more to world history, the Taliban or the collapse of the Soviet empire? Some stirred-up Moslems or the liberation of Central Europe and the end of the Cold War?" His interviewer pursued the subject and asked him, "Some stirred-up Moslems? But isn't Islamic fundamentalism a world menace today?" Mr. Brzezinski replied, "Nonsense! There is no global Islam."[7] How dense can one get?

Greed and Globalization

Coupled with failed foreign policy in dealing with Islamic countries, greed, and politics of oil brought on the problems we face today. Yohani Ramati speaks pointedly to the issue:

> The decision to allow Moslem states to assume full sovereign rights over their oil and natural gas resources and expropriate them in part or sometimes in toto was thus primarily a U.S. gamble based on the hope that these states would cooperate with American oil companies, leaving them effective control and a lion's share of the profits. In practice, effective control passed to the Moslem states concerned, which also appropriated a steadily growing share of the wealth energy produced... The fact that (apart from the U.S. itself) communist USSR and China were the two other biggest oil producers, enabled the Moslems—and particularly the Arabs—to use oil embargoes as a political weapon.[8]

The Arabs have hamstrung our foreign policy by hanging us over a barrel of oil. Fear of an oil embargo which could cripple our economy plays into the hands of the Arabs.

Our Saudi Connection

How is it that the Sheiks of Saudi Arabia are welcome guests at the White House? Do not our leaders know who these people are and what they represent? The Kingdom of Saudi Arabia is the most intolerant Islamic government in the world. The practice of any religion besides Islam is strictly forbidden. While I was in Bangkok, Thailand, recently I met a Filipino who worked in Saudi Arabia for three years. I wanted to find out firsthand from someone who has been there. Here is the interview:

> **Question:** Phillip, why did you choose to work in Saudi Arabia?
> **Answer:** I could earn eight times more money in Saudi Arabia doing the same job as I was doing in the Phillippines.
> **Question:** You were there from 1998 to 2001. How did the Saudi Arabian government treat Christians?
> **Answer:** First, on arrival all personal effects are carefully examined even to examining pictures in wallets. Anything Christian such as a Bible, Christian literature, pictures or symbols, etc., are confiscated. Second, all Christian worship is banned. However, in spite of the ban we clandestinely met in small groups. We sang softly because the religious police actually search for any Christian activity.
> **Question:** Did the religious police catch any of you?
> **Answer:** Yes, several Christian leaders were arrested, threatened with death but were finally sent back to the Philippines. There was also fear that someone could accuse you of blasphemy, i.e., any word or action critical of Islam. This could result in the death penalty.
> **Question:** What in your opinion would happen if Muslims gained control of the Philippines?
> **Answer:** They would outlaw all religions except Islam. It would be very difficult to live and witness for Christ in such a situation.

Saudi Arabia funds the building of three to four mosques a week in our country while thousands of Christians working in Saudi Arabia have no religious freedom at all. Have you ever heard of an uneven playing field like this? Saudi Arabia has 18 million citizens (and 6 million foreign workers). The average Saudi has between six and seven children. In 1981 each family was paid $19,000 and this dole has decreased to $7300 in 1997. At the peak of the oil boon annually $227 billions filled the

Arab coffers. Oil revenue is now down under $50 billion.[9]

Due to failed foreign policy and insatiable greed for money, these billions that were literally donated to the Arabs are funding radical Islam that is threatening the very existence of our nation. Our country desperately needs to free itself from having to please this fanatical Muslim country that is bankrolling Islamic cultural centers around the world, including the United States—that teach hate and provide logistic infrastructure to Islamic terrorism. The same liberals that promote Islam in our schools and society are the same ones who refuse to permit oil wells in Alaska. This insanity must cease.

The Kosovo Conundrum

As usual our diplomats got it all wrong in Bosnia. After the fall of Communism in 1990, the three main ethnic groups formed a coalition government representing the Serbs, Croats, and Muslims. The leader of the Muslim faction reneged on the agreement brokered by the European Union. He opted for unilateral independence and was supported by the U.S. Ambassador in Belgrade, Warren Zimmerman. The fighting and killing in Bosnia was basically a religious war with the Croats, Serbs, and Muslims fighting for power. At the beginning of the conflict, acting Secretary of State Lawrence Eagleburger made it clear that our goal in Bosnia was to mollify the Muslim world and to counter the perception of an anti-Muslim bias regarding American policies in Iraq.[10] The leader of the Muslim nation, Bosnia, was Alija Izetbegovic who "proudly proclaimed in his Islamic Declaration (1974; republished in 1990) that "there can be no peace or coexistence between the Islamic faith and non-Islamic societies and political institutions." He went on to state:

> The Islamic movement should and must start taking power as soon as it is morally and numerically strong enough not only to overthrow the existing non-Islamic power structure, but also to build a great Islamic federation spreading from Morocco to Indonesia, from tropical Africa to Central Asia.[11]

So what happened in Bosnia? Our government demonized the Serbs and glorified the Muslims. Even to this day thousands of our soldiers and millions of our dollars are supporting this country whose sworn and public intent is to destroy non-Islamic countries by a great Islamic federation. How stupid can one's government be?

Pope Appreciates Islam

In a previous chapter we have dealt with this subject. It is a very serious matter that the Roman Catholic Church, which historically has been islamophobic for good reasons, suddenly metamorphs into an islamophile. The pope's acceptance of Islam as a bona fide faith not much different from Judaism and Christianity will aid and abet Muslims to gain strength in non-Muslim countries. To defenders of true Christianity, this is not a good development.

Sudanese Disaster

The dismal failure of our foreign policy is highlighted by the Sudanese tragedy. When the Rt. Rev. Bullen Dolli, Episcopalian bishop from Sudan, came to Washington he was given a very cool reception. He came in October 2001 to talk about the persecution of his flock under Islam. At a scantily attended press conference, the bishop made the following remarks:

> Islam is a militant religion. He pointed out that Sudan's death toll is larger than the combined fatalities suffered in Bosnia, Kosovo, Afghanistan, Chechnya, Somalia and Algeria. Twice as many Sudanese have perished in the past two decades than all the war related deaths suffered by Americans in the past 200 years.[12]

Serge Trifvocic lamented the anti-Christian bias like this:

> But hardly anyone listened. The bishop's host could not get him a slot on NPR or any other of the networks. NPR eagerly accommodates any itinerant mullah praising the Religion of Peace and Tolerance. Poor Bishop Dolli does not understand why the American military has intervened to save the Muslims in Bosnia and Kosovo from alleged genocide perpetrated by their Christian neighbors while it remains indifferent to the very real genocide of Christians that has been perpetrated by the ruling Muslims in Sudan for two decades. He does not understand that his flock's very Christianity barred them from certified victimhood in the eyes of the ruling West-

ern elite.[13]

Unbelievers Get It in the Neck

I was present when Jay Smith, missionary to Muslims in London, England, gave a lecture at Lawrenceville, Georgia, and told about an incident that happened at Cambridge University in England. He was debating two Muslim clerics before an audience of some 300 collegians and faculty. One cleric was a fundamentalist and the other a moderate Muslim. Mr. Smith challenged them with the verse of the Sword:

> Surah 9:5 says, But when the sacred months elapse, then fight and slay the pagan wherever you find them and seize them, besiege them and lie in wait for them in every stratagem of war. But if they repent and establish regular prayers, and practice charity, then open the way for them for Allah is oft-forgiving, Most Merciful.

He then asked them to interpret it. The moderate and the fundamentalist got into a hot exchange as one denied it and the other affirmed it. The fundamental Muslim told Mr. Smith, "yes, the unbelievers will be killed. But Islam is merciful to the People of the Book, i.e., Christian and Jews." Then Mr. Smith turned to that liberal crowd of Christ-bashers and asked, "How many of you are People of the Book?" No hands were raised. "Then if Islam wins England everyone of you will get it in the neck." The audience gasped. Such will be the fate of the ruling Western elite who have rejected the Christ.

End Notes

1. Trifkovic, pp. 279,280.
2. *Brave New School, Islam Studies Required in California District,* WorldNetDaily, 2002, p. 1.
3. Ibid. p. 2.
4. Frum, Linda, *Don't Ask for Me By Name, National Post,* Toronto, October 20, 2002, quoted by Serge Trifkovic, p. 282.
5. Ibid., p. 282.
6. Ibid., p. 209.
7. Interview of National Security Advisor with Le Nouvel Observateur, January, 1998 quoted by Trifvocic, p. 209.
8. Ramatai, Yohanan, *The Islamic Danger to Western Civilization,* Special Publication of the Jerusalem Institute for Western Defense, 2002, pp. 4, 5.
9. Trifkovic, p.246.
10. Eagleburger's *MacNeil/Lehrer PBS NewsHour* interview on October 6, 1992.
11. Trifkovic, p. 218.
12. Ibid., p. 255. Testimony of Roger Winter, Executive Director, U.S. Committee for Refugees on America's Sudan policy to the U.S. House of Representatives on International Relations, March 28, 2001.
13. Ibid.

History is a fascinating subject that suffers much at the hands of historians. In this chapter, we will review the history of Islam with the intent to be perfectly honest. Revisionists (those who change or slant history to their prejudices) can take the facts of history and twist them to their advantage. From my research in writing this book, I have found numerous incidents in which important facts in the history of Islam have been ignored. Two examples are as follows: Yahiya Emerick in his *The Complete Idiot's Guide to Understanding Islam* justifies Mohammed's many wives with the explanation they were old widows that needed someone to care for them[1] and Karen Armstrong in her *A Short History of Islam* portrays Islam as the epitome of tolerance toward both Jews and Christians.[2] It is not my purpose to attack Islam but to state the facts of history.

Skeletons in the Church's Closet

The Christian church's historical record is also sad. The simplicity and spiritual power of New Testament Christianity soon faded as power hungry bishops took over. Study the history of the papacy and you will find two popes ruling at the same time, both claiming to be the Vicar of Christ. Blatant immorality flourished while popes sold indulgences to enrich the coffers of the Church. Think of the "inquisition" when all dissent was cruelly punished with unimaginable torture. Then we note the religious wars of Europe when noble sons were shamelessly sacrificed on the field of battle. Currently we see the Episcopal Church of America ordaining to the office of bishop an immoral, homosexual who left his family to cohabit with a man. The Roman Catholic Church reels as case after case of sexual child abuse are hurled at her priests. Right here I must make a "caveat." All the wickedness mentioned above runs exactly opposite to the character of Jesus Christ and the teachings and principles laid down in Holy Scripture. Let me make an important point: greed, war, immorality, and the like are aberrations in the Christian Church. As we study the history of Islam, the evils are not aberrations but are part and parcel of their founder's character and the teachings of their holy book, the Koran.

Military Nature of Islam

As has been mentioned before, Mohammed started his ministry as the *Rasul*, the messenger of Allah. His stated purpose was to turn people away from idolatry and sinful ways. Following his rejection by the people of Mecca, the Jews, and the Christians, the people of Medina welcomed him and he became their religious, political and military leader. At this time, his *modus operandi* changed from words to swords. The history of Islam is one long, continual battle to conquer the world and bring it forcefully under Muslim rule called *shari'a*.

In this study of the life of Mohammed the capture and slaughter of a Jewish village in Arabia has been described. Muslim convert, Roman Catholic nun Karen Armstrong, explains her view of the situation for us:

> The massacre of the Qurayzah (Arabian Jews) was a horrible incident, but it would be a mistake to judge it by the standards of our own time. This was a very primitive society: the Muslims themselves had just narrowly escaped extermination... In seventh-century Arabia an Arab chief was not expected to show mercy to traitors [anyone who did not accept Islam] like the Quayzah. The executions sent a grim message to Khaybar [a group in Medina who was resisting Mohammed's claims]... The struggle did not indicate any hostility toward Jews in general, but only toward three rebel tribes... Smaller Jewish groups continued to live on in Medina. Later Jews, like Christians, enjoyed full religious liberty in the Islamic empires.[3]

Please see chapter 10 on second class citizens. Our best-selling author goes on to say "anti-semitism is a Christian vice. Hatred of the Jews became marked in the Muslim world only after the creation of the state of Israel."[4] For this lady's information I would direct her to Geisler and Saleeb's book, *Answering Islam—the Crescent in the Light of the Cross,* in which they refer to a Saudi textbook published in A.D. 2000. One lesson is entitled "The Victory of Muslims Over Jews." Read this quote:

> According to tradition from Prophet Mohammed,
> 'The last hour won't come before the Muslims

would fight the Jews and the Muslims will kill
them so Jews would hide behind rocks and trees.
Then the rocks and trees call: oh, Muslim, oh,
servant of God! There is a Jew, behind me, come
and kill him.'[5]

I believe Mohammed lived before the Jews established Israel. Also please see chapter 9 on Islam and Judaism.

John Esposito, an outspoken Islamophile and author of the
massive *Oxford History of Islam,* published by Oxford Press in-
sists that Islam is a religion of peace.[6] Let us see what the Koran
teaches on the subject of war:

Surah 4:74 says, Therefore let those fight in the
way of Allah, who sell this world's life for the
hereafter; and whoever fights in the way of Allah, then be he slain or be he victorious, We shall
grant him a mighty reward.

Surah 5:33 does not indicate that Islam is very peaceful:

The punishment of those who wage war against
Allah and His apostle and strive to make mischief in the land is only this, that they should be
murdered or crucified or their hands and their
feet should be cut off on opposite sides or they
should be imprisoned; this shall be as a disgrace
for them in this world, and in the hereafter they
shall have a grievous chastisement.

Don Richardson in his book, *The Secrets of the Koran,* points
out that there are 109 surahs concerning war.[7] To hold to one's
faith, to protect one's country, and to refuse to accept the sev-
enth-century prophet is to declare war upon Allah and this according to the Koran demands mutilation, death, and Hell.

To understand what Muslim clerics are preaching, let's visit a
mosque in Saudi Arabia and listen. This sermon aired on Riyadh
Kingdom of Saudi Arabia TV in Arabic, official television sta-
tion of the Saudi Government on February 27, 2004 at 0945
GMT from the holy mosque in Mecca. Shaykh Salih Bin-
Muhammad Al Talib delivers the sermon:

O Muslims, and now a final word on the roots. It
is the duty of Muslims to strongly uphold their

religion. The nation of Islam must believe that it is the only one on the right path, that Islam is the last of religions, that the Koran is the last of the Books and most importantly, that Prophet Muhammad, may the peace and blessings of God be upon him, is the last of the apostles, that the Islamic law [*shari'a*] is a copy of their laws, and that God will not accept any other religion. Thus, it is impermissible to concede any of that **even if at the cost of our lives.** We say this at a time when some defeatists have weakened and called for mixing distorted scriptures with Islamic religion under the claim of bringing religions closer to one another. We say it also at a time when some people's faith is so weak as to believe that everyone is correct.

This began from the statements uttered by some and the behavior and theses written by others. It is as if they did not hear God's words:

"If anyone desires a religion other than Islam, never it will be accepted of him; and in the Hereafter he will be in the ranks of those who have lost." If we are to renew the religious discourse, we must go back to the roots. This means going back to the Koran and the Sunnah.[8] *(author's emphasis)*

Modern Wars with Muslim Killing Muslim

In 1947, Great Britain gave India its independence and divided the country between the Hindus and the Muslims. Since a great proportion of the people living in the Punjab State in the west of India and in East Bengal in the east of India were Muslims, an Islamic nation was created with two provinces. The two provinces were East and West Pakistan separated by 1000 miles of Indian territory. In 1971, political turmoil erupted in these two provinces. West Pakistan sent 80,000 Pakistani soldiers (99% Muslims) to East Pakistan with a simple order: kill Bengalis. 85% of East Pakistanis were Muslims and in a few short months one million Bengali Muslims and Hindus were killed and ten million took refuge in India.[9] To stop the carnage and relieve themselves of ten million unwanted refugees, India declared war and defeated West Pakistan. As a result, the nation of Bangladesh was born. Muslims killed Muslims without mercy.

The Key to Heaven

The Iran-Iraq eight-year war is another sad example of Muslim killing Muslim. Iran's Ayatollah Khomeini was a Shiite Muslim and Iraq's Suddam Hossain is a Sunni Muslim. As has been mentioned before, Shiites and Sunnis don't like one another. Whatever their motivation, these two nations fiercely fought each other for eight years with a million dead. Again, the story of Muslim killing Muslim. Khomeini went on television asking for 10,000 young volunteers to fight against Iraq and become *basijis,* those who were committed to die. A red piece of tape was put on their foreheads. They volunteered to clear the minefields, and the military leaders would send out 5,000 boys to run through the mine fields to trip the mines. Others were ordered to throw themselves on high voltage border fences. Thousands of young boys died in this way. To them Khomeini gave the promise of *beheste, (heaven).* To symbolize this promise he gave them a key to hang around their necks— a key, which could open the gates of heaven.[10] This is part of the sad history of Islam. Someone will say, "But they are bad Muslims." I will say, "Yes, but they are Muslims." Furthermore, in his book, *Islamic Rule,* Khomeini clearly identifies his ideologies, claims, and views as a revival of a tradition he traces to Mohammed, the Prophet of Islam.[11] The Muslim Brotherhood in Egypt and Syria are not Shiites but Sunnis, and they are violent, bloodthirsty men. They trained their young members for jihad against the British colonialists and others. Their slogan was "The Koran is our constitution, the Prophet is our guide; death for the glory of Allah is our greatest ambition."[12]

Proud Parents

Below is the sad account of a Muslim family's testimony after their daughter killed herself and 19 others.

> A day after she killed 19 people at a restaurant in the port city of Haifa, the parents of a Palestinian suicide bomber said Sunday that they were proud of their daughter because she had avenged the death of her brother. Hanadi Jaradat, 27,

worked as an apprentice lawyer. Her parents said she was a devout Muslim. The unmarried woman had witnessed the death of her brother, Fadi Jaradat, during an Israeli army operation in Jenin on June 12. Both were members of the radical Palestinian Islamic Jihad movement.

'She was deeply upset as she was very close to her brother,' said her mother, Umm Fadi. 'I am happy with her because she has killed those who have killed my son. They kill us everyday.' In response to the bombing, the Israeli army destroyed the family's home early Sunday... On Sunday, as the Al-Jazeera Arab satellite channel played a video of Jaradat shortly before she embarked on her suicide mission, her father, Taysse Jaradat, described his pride. 'She is a very strong person,' he said. In a statement claiming responsibility for the attack the Islamic Jihad said it was a response 'to the Israeli crimes which continue against our people.'[13]

To civilized people this is exceedingly sad.

Slavery and Islam

Slavery is a fact of life in both the Old and New Testaments. However, it is never recognized as a divine institution, but a thing of man. The early Christians never made a big issue of slavery, but the outworking of a Christian ethic sounded the death knoll for slavery. Slavery was finally abolished in England, and to end this travesty against humanness, Americans fought a bloody war. The Koran, by contrast, not only assumes slavery's existence, but also regulates its practice in considerable detail and therefore endows it with divine sanction. Mohammed and his companions owned slaves, or acquired them in war. Mohammed's Koran recognizes the basic inequality between master and slave and the rights of the former over the latter. The Koran assures Muslims the right to own slaves (to "possess their necks") either by purchasing them or as a bounty of war. Ibn Timiya, an Islamic historian wrote, "Slavery is justified because of the war itself; however, it is not permissible to enslave a free Muslim. It is lawful to kill the infidel or to enslave him, and it also makes it lawful to take his offspring into captivity."[14] The slave trade inside the Islamic Empire and along its edges was vast. It began to flourish at the time of the Muslim expansion into Africa, in the middle of the seventh century, and it still survives today in Mauritania, Saudi Arabia, and Sudan. Fortunate for Arabs being "the noblest of all races" they were exempt from enslavement [15]

During the heyday of the Ottoman Empire, the Muslims practiced *devshirme*. Christian fathers were forced to appear in the town squares with their sons, the strongest and brightest of whom would be seized from their parents, converted to Islam and trained to be part of the empire's crack fighting force, the janissaries.[16]

Lack of Freedom

Observing the fruits of Islam and Muslim communities, one will realize that Islam's strongest weapon is fear. Imagine the fear that gripped the hearts of the Arabs on hearing Surah 9:5, "When the sacred months are past, kill those who join other gods wherever you find them, and lie in wait for them with every kind of ambush; but if they convert and observe prayer and pay the obligatory alms, let them go their way." Very forceful motivation for becoming a Muslim, I would say. Submit or die! Not only is one forced to become a Muslim, but once a Muslim always a Muslim. In the *Bill of Legal Punishment* published by the Azhar University in Cairo—the "Light of Islam" accepted as the highest authority of *shari'a*— has been widely circulated in English among the Muslim diaspora. Notice what it says about apostasy:

> A person guilty of apostasy (man or woman) shall
> be put to death if repentance is not made within
> the period allowed which shall not exceed sixty
> days... An apostate is that Muslim who has re-
> nounced the faith of Islam irrespective of his
> adoption of another creed. Apostasy is renun-
> ciation of Islam by act or statement; denial of
> essential tenets of the faith; and bringing into
> ridicule through word or action the Gracious
> Koran.[17]

There never has been a mass exodus from Islam. The reason is not that Islam is so great or appealing, or successful, but those trapped in it cannot escape.

Salman Rushdie Affair

Salmon Rushdie is a British Muslim author who twenty-four years ago wrote a book, *Satanic Verses,* which was critical of the Koran. Ayatollah Khomeini of Iran put out a *fatwah*, an official Islamic statement demanding the death of Rushdie. The fatwah instructs Muslims throughout the world to assassinate Rushdie. The strangest phenomenon in this saga was not Khomenie's *fatwah,* but the failure of the liberals and moderate Muslims to come to his defense. Rushdie was not praised for exercising his freedom of speech, but was criticized for "stirring up a hornet's nest."[18] So far Rushdie has escaped the wrath of his enemies.

Women's Rights in Islam

Our converted nun, Karen Armstrong, tells us that emancipation of women was a project dear to the Prophet's heart.[19] The best way to show her error and prejudice is to simply go to their holy book, the Koran.

Men are superior to women:
Surah 2:228 says,

> And the divorced women should keep themselves in waiting for three courses; and it is not lawful for them that they should conceal what Allah has created in their wombs, if they believe in Allah and the last day; and their husbands have a better right to take them back in the meanwhile if they wish for reconciliation; and they have rights similar to those against them in a just manner, and **the men are a degree above them,** and Allah is Mighty, Wise. *(author's emphasis)*

This superiority is divinely ordained:

> Sura 4:34 says, Men are the maintainers of women because Allah has made some of them **to excel others** and because they spend out of their property; the good women are therefore obedient, guarding the unseen as Allah has guarded; and (as to) those on whose part you fear desertion, admonish them, and leave them alone in the sleeping-places and **beat them;** then if they obey you, do not seek a way against them;

surely Allah is High, Great. *(author's emphasis)*

According to the Koran men are a little smarter than women.

> Surah 2:282 says, "Call in two male witnesses from among you, but if two men cannot be found, then **one man and two women whom you judge fit to act as witnesses; so that if either of them commit an error, the other will remember**." *(author's emphasis)*

According to tradition recorded by Islamic historians the Prophet said, "Then I stood at the gate of the Fire and saw that the majority of those who entered it were women."[20] Yes, women were very dear to the Prophet's heart!

As for women's rights U.S. Department of State's Country *Report on Human Rights Practices in the Kingdom of Saudi Arabia* for A.D. 2000 gives some startling facts. "Women must not drive cars, and must not be driven, except by an employee, or husband, or a close relative—and then must not occupy the front seat... The authorities monitor any gatherings of persons, especially women, and disperse women found in public places such as restaurants. Women may study abroad—but only at the undergraduate level—if accompanied by a spouse or an immediate male relative. Women own 4 percent of the businesses, but they must deputize a male relative to represent the business."[20]

America: Patron of Islam

In writing the above unfavorable aspects of Islam, this author has scrupulously avoided conjecture, opinion, or hearsay and has stuck to the facts. Our ruling elite, George W. Bush included, either does not know the facts or has chosen to look the other way. In fact, the U.S. government distances itself from every day people who watch the news and associate Islam with violence. According to Milam, "there are unfortunately some ill-informed... Americans who fear Islam... [who] confuse Islam with terrorism. I can tell you, without fear of contradiction, that the U.S. government does not share that confusion.[21] In fact, the government has gone all out to promote understanding, dialogue and exchange. A Department of State fact sheet sees a remedy "through education, people-to-people exchanges, and by encouraging responsible reporting in the mass media and accurate portrayal in the movie industry."[22] Along with me, you are probably wondering what is behind this error on the part of our government. Why go to such lengths to pronounce Islam a faith completely unblemished by the violence of some of its practitioners?

Daniel Pipes gives us the answer:

> This exercise (favoring Islam) has a patently prac-tical objective: it is designed to lessen Muslim hostility to the United States. The chain of rea-soning goes as follows: (1) Many Muslims crave Western respect for Islam and the recognition of its virtues. (2) The U.S. government in turn yearns for acceptance by Muslims. (3) Therefore, Washington gives Muslims the acceptance they seek. (4) Grateful Muslims diminish their hostil-ity to the United States. (5) Washington can real-istically demand that those same Muslims come to the defense of the United States against the more radical Muslims who still oppose it. (In addition, some of this rhetoric serves domestic purposes to assuage the U.S. Muslim popula-tion.)[23]

Bill Clinton said, "Islam is American as apple pie."[24] I think he does not know much about America or Islam. America's basic values are individualism, freedom, rule of law based on our Constitution and the law of God (Ten Commandments), democracy, and the ownership of private property. Islam is absolutist with not one shred of freedom to the human spirit. Submit or die! Our government's attitude toward Islam has se-rious implications. Their scolding of citizens that tell the truth about Islam and their noisy espousal of Islam's virtues causes our government to be an apologete for Islam making it an ad-junct to Islamic organizations. As Mr. Pipes says,

> By dismissing any connection between Islam and terrorism, complaining about media distortion, and claiming America needs Islam, they have turned the U.S. government into a discreet mis-sionary of the faith. Without anyone quite real-izing it, the resources of the federal government have been deployed to help Muslims spread their message, and, in effect their faith. If the "war on

terror" is to have any larger purpose, it must free people from the yoke of politicized Islam. There can be no better place to begin than right at home.[25]

Bush Administration Yielding to Muslim Pressure

The Council on American Islamic Relations (CAIR) is bombarding the Whitehouse with e-mails and the Bush administration is yielding by actively supporting Islam. U.S. tax dollars are funding Muslim Madrasas (elementary schools) in Indonesia. Not only this, but a one million dollar grant of our tax money is being offered to Evangelical seminaries to offer a "politically correct" course on Islam. *The Los Angeles Times* had this to say:

The action of the Bush administration over the weekend has potential to create a problem for Fuller Theological Seminary and its president, Richard Mouw. One of the nation's leading evangelical Christian seminaries has launched a federally funded project for making peace with Muslims, featuring a proposed code of ethics that rejects offensive statements about each other's faiths, affirms a mutual belief in one God, and pledges not to proselytize."[26]

Mr. Lingerfelter of the department of Justice calls this "conflict resolution. The program, characterized by the Department of Justice as "a conflict resolution program" in its $993,500 grant, is intended largely "to lead a large portion of evangelical Christians into a better understanding of Islam," he said. "After 9/11 there was a great deal of hostility in the Christian community toward Muslims. It is important for Christians to gain a respect for them and treat them with dignity and not assume they're all terrorists."[27]

Missionary statesman and noted author, Don Richardson has interesting insights into our government's espousing Islam.

Premise: Osama bin Laden wants nothing more than to promote Islam universally, yet he launches a terrorist war that entails a terrible risk of discrediting Islam universally and irrepa-rably. Still, a masterfully ingenius plot lies hid-den in his madness. Here is what Osama bin Laden foresees:

1) President Bush retaliates with a war against Muslim terrorists.

2) Millions of Muslims already embedded in Western nations plead vociferously—in concert with always-blame-America-first Western liber-als—that Islam is innocent and that Bush's war on terror, by implications discredits Islam.

3) Osama bin Laden guesses that George Bush's tender Christian conscience will cause him to overreach trying to avoid hurting the feelings of 1.3 billion Muslims. Massively affirming Islam at home and worldwide while continuing his war against Islam-based terror, Bush leads billions of people who formerly found Islam suspect to per-ceive it—in spite of Osama bin Laden (yet also, in a twisted sense, because of him)—as a good religion.

4) End result: Osama bin Laden wins by achiev-ing his primary goal in the end game! George Bush and the free world, in spite of the war on terror, lose by unwittingly strengthening a reli-gion that aims ultimately to impose Sharia Law across the free world. And Sharia Law, be assured, is the antithesis of democracy!

So—the veterinarian who aspired to remove a wart from a crocodile's nose ends up in its jaws.[28]

End Notes

1. Emerick. P. 285.
2. Armstrong, p. 21.
3. Ibid.
4. Ibid.
5. Geisler and Saleed, p. 328.
6. Exposito, p. 631.
7. Richardson, p. 28.
8. WWW.GAMLA.COM, website defending Israel
9. *Time, Pakistan: Toppling Over the Brink,* April 5, 1971, pp. 18. 19.
10. Safa, Reza, *Inside Islam—A Former Shiite Muslim Speaks Out,* Charisma House, Lake Mary, Fl. 1996, p. 41.
11. Ibid., p. 43.

12. Ibid., p. 44.
13. Jenin, West Bank USA Today Oct. 8, 2003, Nasser Abu Bakr.i
14. Timiyya, Ibn, Vol. 31. p. 380.
15. Trifkovic, p. 172.
16. Spencer, Herbert, *Islam Unveiled,* Encounter Books, San Francisco, CA. 2002, p. 32.
17. Trifkovic, p. 150.
18. Warraq, Ibn, *Why I Am Not A Muslim,* Prometheus Books, Amherst, NY, 1995, p. 9.
19. Armstrong, p. 16.
20. Bukhari, Sahih, vol. 1, bk. 67, no. 5196.
21. Trifkovic, p. 154
22. *"U.S is against terrorism Not Islam,"* English Speaking Union of Lahore, quoted by Pipes, p. 101
23. "Fact sheet" *U.S. Government Views on Terrorism,* quoted by Pipes, p. 101.
24. Pipes, p. 101.
25. Ibid., p. 103.
26. *Los Angeles Times,* December 21, 2003
27. Ibid.
28. E-mail from Don Richardson, December 9, 2003.

During the passing of time, God has used key men to change the course of history. Moses delivered his people from the bondage of Egypt. God used Samuel to prepare the way for David's kingdom. Judas Macabee and his sons victoriously defied the armies of Antiochus Epiphanes. Charles Martel and his brave soldiers saved the world from Islam. While Chamberlain succumbed to Hitler's subterfuges, Winston Churchill stepped in to save the free world from Fascism. More recently when the red tide of Communism threatened to engulf all of Europe and the world, Ronald Reagan had the courage to call the USSR an evil empire. His courageous leadership breathed hope into European countries that ultimately resulted in the collapse of the Iron Curtain. Who will be the man God uses to rescue the world from the clutches of Islam? Is it George W. Bush? Only God knows.

Is Anybody Listening?

Americans have a bad habit of not taking the threats of our enemies seriously. The Chairman of the Council on American-Islamic Relations, Omar M. Ahmad, told a crowd of California Muslims in July, 1998, "Islam isn't in America to be equal to any other faith, but to become dominant. The Koran.... should be the highest authority in America and Islam the only accepted religion on Earth."[1] How clearer can the goal of islamizing America be stated? The ramifications from Mr. Ahmad's statement are horrifying. Our constitutional rights would disappear and all of us who name the name of Christ would be *dhimmis,* second class citizens stripped of our dignity and freedom that we learned about earlier.

Islam More Than a Religion

The majority of Americans believe that Islam is just one of the world's great religions bringing peace and comfort to those who happen to adhere to the Muslim faith. An article, *The Islamic Agenda,* taken from www.answeringislam.org says the following:

> It is indeed a religion but it is fatal to stop there. The heart of Islamic teaching is that religion is not just a part of life, but life is a tiny part of

religion. As such, Islam is a system that is socio-political, socio-religious, socio-economic, educational, legislative, judicial, and militaristic.[2]

Since an American Muslim is part of a system that is much more than just a religion, Dr. Anis Shorrosh, a Christian Arab who is an authority on Islam, contends that a Muslim cannot be a good American. He says,

> Theologically, no. Because his allegiance is to Allah, the moon god of Arabia.
> Scripturally, no. Because his allegiance is to the five pillars of Islam and the Quran.
> Geographically, no. Because his allegiance is to Mecca, to which he turns in prayer five times a day.
> Socially, no. Because his allegiance to Islam forbids him to make friends with Christians or Jews.
> Politically, no. Because he must submit to the mullahs (spiritual leaders), who teach the annihilation of Israel and the destruction of America, the Great Satan.
> Domestically, no. Because he is permitted to have four wives and beat and scourge them when disobedient. Surah 4:34.
> Religiously, no. Because no other religion is accepted by Allah—intolerance. Surah 2:256.
> Intellectually, no. Because he cannot accept the American Constitution since it is based on Biblical principles and he believes the Bible to be corrupt.
> Philosophically, no. Because Islam, Mohammed, and the Quran do not allow freedom of religion and expression. Democracy and Islam cannot coexist. Every Muslim government is either dictatorial or autocratic.
> Spiritually, no. Because when we declare "one nation under God" the Christian's God is loving and kind, while Allah is never referred to as our heavenly Father, nor is he ever called love in the Quran's 99 excellent names of Allah.[3]

The theme of this book is telling the truth. The simple truth is that Islam grants Muslims a mandate. It is a mandate to change the existing free, democratic society into an Islamic society. It is to make Islam supreme and thus dominate every aspect of society. This is not only the desire of the fundamentalists like Osama bin Laden, but from their preaching and publications it would seem to be the desire of Muslims worldwide.

Saudi Incursion in America

Of the more than 1200 mosques in America, more than 80 percent have been built with Saudi money. Saudi Arabia alone has spent $87 billion since 1973 to spread Islam throughout the United States and the Western hemisphere.[4] For example, King Fahd of Saudi pledged $8 million to build a new mosque at the Masjid Bilal Islamic Center in South Central Los Angeles. This mosque is associated with the Black Muslim American Society. Each major city has one main mosque and two or three smaller centers in the suburbs. Saudis are embracing "Wahabbism," an acute and violent strain of Islam. Osama bin Laden considers himself a "Wahabbi." So one has every reason to believe that what is being taught in these mosques and Islamic centers supported by Saudi Arabia is Wahabbism. Black converts make up the fastest-growing segment of the Muslim population in America. An estimated 60 to 90 percent of all U.S. converts to Islam are black. *Christianity Today* predicts that if the conversion rates continue, Islam could become the dominant religion in black urban areas by 2020.[5]

Danger is Real

My fear is not of America being bombed or terrorized. Of course, this is always a possibility. However, our enemies are not stupid and they learned that bombing America will hinder rather than aid their cause. Attacking our people would mobilize them and put American Muslims under severe pressure. No, I'm quite sure the current plan is to present Islam as a great religion, a moral force which fights crime, abortion, pornography, and gambling, and at the same time multiply the influence of Islam by immigration, reproduction and conversion. As the numbers of Muslims increase what has happened in France, Germany and England will happen here. In Germany, the number of Muslim residents is reaching 3 million and the number of mosques exceeds 2000 and voices of warning are being heard:

> The Turks (Muslims) in Berlin constitute a so-
> cial problem without a solution. There are en-
> tire sections of the city closed in on themselves
> that support a parallel and hostile culture, with
> no kind of symbiosis with the German culture.
> And the Magrebins (Muslims) have done the
> same thing in Marseilles [France]. The very op-
> posite of integration, their objective is to orga-
> nize a society according to the Kuran. Islam is a
> way of life that annuls any separation between
> the religious, civil, and political reality.[6]

Serge Trifvocic writes:

> In France and all over Europe demands are pre-
> sented for businesses employing Muslims to ob-
> serve the Islamic calendar, or for the state schools
> to be segregated by sex and include the tenets of
> Islam in the curriculum. Everywhere they de-
> mand the wearing of the *hijab*, the traditional
> headscarf. Anyone refusing their demands is
> immediately branded "racist" and an example of
> government intolerance.[7]

In the days ahead the same phenomena will happen in America.

The Times of India gave the following statistics on Muslim growth in Great Britain:

> The number of Muslims in Great Britain who
> worship weekly has overtaken the number of
> Anglicans doing the same. 930,000 Muslims at-
> tend a mosque weekly, while just 916,000 Angli-
> cans can be found in church each week. Over
> sixteen million Britons, about a quarter of the
> population, claim affiliation with the Church of
> England.[8]

What Can the Government Do?

If you are a discerning reader, you will have learned that the current global Islamic threat is due to wrong-headed American foreign policy. Some changes must be made. First, our government needs to understand that Islam is more than just a religion by its own admission. Its oft stated aim is to replace our democratic process with Islam's *shari'a* or rule. Since treason and overthrow of our social order is preached in their mosques and Islamic centers, they need to be understood and subjected to the same supervision and legal restraints that apply to other cults prone to violence, and to violent political hate groups whose avowed aim is the destruction of our order of life.

Second, our government should diligently protect human rights around the world. As we have learned in an earlier chapter, our nation's policy has been to protect the persecuted Muslims and to forget the persecuted Christians. This must stop. Those countries that insist on killing and enslaving their Christian minorities must be dealt with by diplomatic and economic sanctions. If this is not successful, then military action must be taken. In Indonesia, "Amnesty International estimates that Indonesia had murdered 200,000 East Timorese, out of a population of 600,000-700,000."[9] The same estimate was given by the Human Rights Watch in 1989. This is worse carnage than Pol Pot's in Cambodia. Where was the outcry? Our government knew but chose to do nothing.

Third, our dependence upon Arab oil is immoral. Despite Saudi Arabia's growing anti-American extremism, attempts to reduce U.S. dependence on Saudi oil have fallen flat. America imports more than half its oil supply, and Saudi is the biggest overseas supplier, shipping more than 1.5 million barrels here a day, according to the American Petroleum Institute. Bush's energy plan to open up Alaska wilderness reserve to oil drilling was killed by Democrats and a handful of eco-friendly Republicans. How insane and unpatriotic! Curiously, the initiative went down without more than a whimper from the White House. This source of oil could produce and estimated 6 to 16 billion barrels of domestic crude—potentially replacing all of what America imports from the Saudis.[10]

Fourth, the INS (Immigration Naturalization Service) needs revamping. They seem to let in the bad people in and keep out the good people. Applicants from Muslim countries that are hostile to the United States should not be given entry visas. Our borders should be protected by the military. Illegal immigrants must be arrested and deported. All of these measures are scorned by the political correct crowd but are essential for the survival of our Republic.

Fifth, a "long-term counterterrorist strategy must entail denying Islam a foothold inside" America. David Pryce-Jones, the British writer put it this way: "Democracy sometimes appears paralyzed by those who take advantage of its freedoms in order to abuse them for undemocratic ends."[11]

Muslims Persecute Christians

"Evil triumphs when good men do nothing." Two men were arguing which was the worse evil, ignorance or apathy. A third man joined in saying, "I don't know and I don't care." Ignorance and apathy are certainly our two worst enemies. My purpose in writing this book is to inform people of the truth—not what I say the Muslims say but to show exactly what they say in their own words. America needs to know what is happening in Indonesia, as Muslims are killing Christians and burning churches with impunity. Nobody seems to care.

In October 2003, Hridoy Roy, a 27-year old Bengali Christian evangelist showed the *Jesus Film* in a Muslim village at the request of the village leader. Late in the night while walking home, seven Muslims stabbed him to death. In Lebanon a Muslim man shot and killed a missionary wife for teaching children about Jesus. In Yemen three Southern Baptist medical missionaries were shot to death in their clinic by a Muslim man. In Murree, Pakistani Muslim militants attacked a Christian school. They killed several Muslim watchmen. The students escaped certain death by hiding behind locked doors. The school has been closed. Both Nigeria and Sudan are facing fierce persecution by Muslim governments.

Closer to home in Virginia Beach, VA an Afghan Muslim has been converted to Christ through kindness shown to him after an accident by members of a church. In the land of the free this new Christian is now hiding in fear of being killed by an American Islamic group. The liberal news media does not consider this news worth telling. The media is suppressing and holding down the truth. The American people must be made aware of the slaughter of thousands of Christians around the world and threats against those who turn to Christ from Islam in America.

Question for American Muslims

Thousands of Muslims have fled their homelands to enjoy the freedom, prosperity and opportunity that America affords.

In interviews with U.S. Immigration officials, they complain about the lack of freedom in their home country, citing specific instances in the areas of human rights and politics. But as soon as they gain permanent residence, let alone citizenship, they turn against their host nation and begin to praise the virtues of an Islamic state. You American Muslim, do you not realize that millions of American are God-fearing, moral, love their families, work hard, do not drink alcohol or smoke, pay their taxes and have built the greatest country in the history of the human race? Do you not also realize that the American people welcomed you into their society, trusting you to be loyal to your adopted homeland? Does not your own conscience tell you it is wrong to seek to destroy the people who have received you as one of their own? When earthquakes devastate Muslim Turkey or any other country, who rushes to their aid? Saudi Arabia with its fabulous income of $270 billion in 1980? No, it is the *kafirs,* the infidels from America that come to their aid. The heart of Islam is Saudi Arabia. For the past 50 years due to American technology and ingenuity they are one of the richest countries in the world. If Islam has the answer for the problems of the world, would you not think that Saudi Arabia, the womb of Islam, would be a world leader in such areas as education, ethics, human rights, technology, military? Would you not think that Saudi Arabia could have made life better for the poor refugees in Palestine? American Muslim, can you show me one Islamic country better than America? If America is so wicked, why do Muslims want to live here? Why don't you choose to live in some Muslim country? American Muslim, I have asked you some hard questions, but now I want to give you some straight answers. Americans are good and generous as a people, but we will fight for our freedoms, our faith, and our Bible. We will fight for your freedom to be a Muslim. But we will fight you if you try to rob us of our freedom and to make Islam and the Koran dominant in America. This is a Christian country built by Christian people, and we plan to keep it that way, God helping us. American Muslim, if you agree with this, we are happy for you to stay and be one of us. But if you insist on the overthrow of our democratic republic for religious reasons or whatever, you are persona non gratis (unwelcome). In other words, get out!

Revival of Biblical Christianity

A spiritual battle is raging between the cross and the crescent. In England the apostasy has done its deadly work among the churches. Buildings that used to be churches are nightclubs, Hindu temples and Muslim mosques. The Washington Times quotes a Pakistani-born Anglican who grew up as a Muslim to this effect: "In Britain today, where Islam controls the inner cities, we have major social exclusion and the development of *Shari'a* (Muslim government). We have had churches burned, Christians attacked, and a mission center destroyed. The media has deliberately kept this off the air."[12] At a Pastors' Fellowship, someone made the statement that in America every week 48 churches close and four new mosques are built.

Where there is a spiritual vacuum, error quickly fills the void. Jean Raspail, author of *Camp of the Saints,* a fictional story of an Asian takeover in France, made this statement in his preface:

> The West is empty, even if it has not yet become really aware of it. An extraordinary inventive civilization, surely the one capable of meeting the challenges of the third millennium, the West has no soul left. At every level—it is always the soul that wins the decisive battles.[13]

This loss of soul in the West is evidenced in nihilism, humanism, secularism, agnosticism, multiculturalism, religious diversity (all religions are good and true), denial of absolute truth, and post-modernism. In this sort of environment, Islam flourishes because without a doubt, it has a soul, a conviction, a will, and a claim—there is no god but Allah and Mohammed is his prophet. The only power that can stop Islam is Biblical Christianity. Our great nation with its high ideals of freedom, the worth of the individual, man's inalienable right to pursue life, liberty, and happiness came from Judeo-Christian values. The West that has lost its soul is the West that has turned it back on the Bible. The ruling Western elite has rejected the God of heaven (see Psalm 2) and to spite Him and His followers they are promoting Islam. Liberal academics and opinion-makers [who] sympathize with Islam partly because it is a leading historical rival of the Western civilization they hate and partly because they long for a romanticized and sanitized Muslim past that substitutes for the authentic Western and Christian roots they have rejected.

America is in Trouble

Attorney David Gibbs, Jr. in his article *When I Think Of America in 2003* makes us think deeply as to our future and the kind of America our grandchildren and great-grandchildren will live in. He says:

> When I think of America, I remember a nation where morality was once defined in the pulpits and was encouraged by the Congress and all fifty state legislatures. I remember a nation where compassionate, committed individuals honored God and cared for each other and their communities. I remember a nation where Americans believed in the Word of God and were committed to following the principles established therein. I remember an America where the church provided the societal values to build strong families, communities and governments.[14]

In this excellent article in *The Legal Alert,* Attorney Gibbs with stunning statistics catalogs how America has fallen. He writes of the breakdown of the family, alcoholism, sexual abuse, violence, and a media filled with unbridled sexual content. Today, there is an increasing advocacy for a "diverse" society that not only encourages immoral behavior but also seeks to quiet all Christian opposition to such immorality. As Christians, we cannot allow hostility toward Christianity to silence us. Rather such criticism should embolden us to proclaim the truth of God's Word. To save our country from this "wicked diversity," Bible-believing Christians need to commit themselves to the following: pray that God will bless us again in America with a true revival; do all that we can to win others (including Muslims) to Christ; strongly hold our Biblical standards and values in our churches and pulpits; stay involved in our national, state, and local governments as an influence for good and for God; and raise and educate our own children and our church's children to honor and revere God and His Holy Word.[15]

More Sure Word of Prophecy

Looking at conditions from our human worldly viewpoint we see a situation that is not pleasant. The Church of Jesus Christ in America is not healthy. Christians are the "punching bags" that the "shakers and movers" punch with no fear of incrimination. Judicial fiat has outlawed the God of the Bible from public and "boxed" Him in the churches. Neo-evangelicalism has run its course and is no longer evangelical. Christian fundamentalists view each other with suspicion. The super churches are no longer soul-winning churches with bus routes. Seeker friendly churches giving people what they want instead of what they need are the biggies today. Instead of the Church going into the world with the Gospel today, the world is coming into the Church with entertainment.

The Church, the body, may be weak but the Head is very strong. Consider Martin Luther's words:

> Did we in our own strength confide, Our striving would be losing:
> Were not the right Man on our side, The Man of God's own choosing. Dost ask who that may be? Christ Jesus it is He; Lord Sabaoth is His name, From age to age the same, And He must win the battle.[16]

Yes! He must win the battle! Islam has no prophecy of any intent. The Holy Bible gives us great details of what is going to happen in the future. Every prophecy concerning Christ's first coming has been literally fulfilled. Every prophecy concerning His Second Coming will be literally fulfilled. Those of you whose hearts may be afraid after reading the *Peril of Islam,* let these verses bring peace to your hearts.

> And to **you who are troubled rest with us,** *when the Lord Jesus shall be revealed from heaven with his mighty angels, in flaming fire taking vengeance on them that know not God, and that obey not the gospel of our Lord Jesus Christ: Who shall be punished with everlasting destruction from the presence of the Lord, and from the glory of his power* (II Thessalonians 2:7-9). (*Author's emphasis.*)

That prophecy brings rest to a troubled heart. Let this promise put a spring in your step.

> *Wherefore God also hath highly exalted him, and*

given him a name which is above every name: That
at the name of Jesus every knee should bow, of things
in heaven, and things in earth, and things under
the earth; and that every tongue should confess that
Jesus Christ is Lord, to the glory of God the Father
(Philippians 2:9-11).

What is going to transpire between now and then we do not know. But this we do know: truth is mightier than the sword. Islam depends on the sword to make converts and to keep converts. The one who is the Truth said, *"Fear not; I am the first and the last: I am he that liveth, and was dead; and, behold, I am alive for evermore, Amen; and have the keys of hell and death"* (Revelation 1:17b-18). All is well that ends well.

End Notes:

1. Report in *San Ramon Valley Herald* of a speech to California Muslims in July 1998; quoted by Daniel Pipes on *CAIR: Moderate Friends of Terror,* *New York Post,* April 22, 2002.
2. *The Islamic Agenda and Its Blueprints, Evangelicals Now,* March 2002, p.1.
3. Shorrosh, Anis, *Can a Muslim be a Good American?,* copied from a handout.
4. Sperry, Paul, *U.S.-Saudi Oil Imports Fund American Mosques, WorldNetDaily,* april 22, 2002, p. 2.
5. Ibid., pp. 2, 3.
6. Trifkovic, p. 288.
7. Ibid., p. 289.
8. *Times of India,* england.anglican.org, January 25, 2004.
9. Ibid. p. 213.
10. Sperry, Paul, pp. 6, 7.
11. Pryce-Jones, David
12. Safa, Reza, *Inside Islam—Exposing and Reaching the World of Islam,* Charisma House, Lake Mary FL., 1996, p. 52.
13. Raspail, Jean, *The Camp of the Saints,* The Social Contract Press, Petoskey, MI, 1973, p. xv.
14. Gibbs, David, Jr., *When I Think of America in 2003,* Legal Alert, pp. 1, 2.
15. Ibid.
16. Luther, Martin, *A Mighty Fortress is Our God, Favorite Hymns of Praise,* Tabernacle Publishing Company, Wheaton, IL, 1978, p. 466.

BIBLIOGRAPHY

American Jihad—The Terrorists Living Among Us, Steven Emerson, The Free Press, New York, 2002.

Answering Islam, The Crescent in Light of the Cross, Norman Geisler and Abdul Saleeb, Baker Books, Grand rapids, MI, 2002.

Behind the Veil—Unmasking Islam, Abd el Schafi, Pioneer Book Company, Caney, Ks, 2001.

Fast Facts on the Middle East Conflict, Randall Price, Harvest House Publishers, Eugene, Oregon, 2003

Inside Islam, Exposing and Reaching The World of Islam, Reza Safa, Charisma House, Lake Mary, FL., 1996.

Islam—a Short History, Karen Armstrong, The Modern Library, New York, 2000.

Islam, a User Friendly Guide, Bruce Bickel and Stan Jantz, Harvest House Publishers, Eugene, Or, 2002.

Islam & Christianity, Donald Tingle, Inter-Varsity Press, Madison, Wisconsin, 1985.

Islam and the Jews—The Unfinished Battle, Mark Gabriel, Charisma House, Lake Mary FL., 2003.

Islam and Terrorism- What the Quran Really Teaches About Christianity, Violence and the Goals of the Islamic Jihad, Mark Gabriel, Charisma House, Lake Mary, Fl., 2002.

Islam in History—Ideas, People, and Events in the Middle East, Bernard Lewis, Open Court, Chicago and La Salle, IL, 1993

Islam: Its Prophet, Peoples, Politics and Power, George Brawell, Jr., Broadman and Holman Publishers, Nashville, TN, 1996.

Islam Revealed—A Christian Arab's View of Islam, Anis Shorrosh, Thomas Nelson Publishers, Nashville, TN, 1988.

Islam Unveield—Disturbing Questions About the Worlds Fastest Growing Faith, Robert Spencer, Encounter Books, Sans Francisco, CA, 2002.

Islamic Invasion—Confronting the World's Fastest Growing Religion, Robert Morey, Christian Scholars Press, Las Vegas, NV, 1992.

Jesus, Prophecy and Middle East, Anis Shorrosh, Acclaimed Books, Dallas, TX, 1979.

A Cup of Trembling—Jerusalem and Bible Prophecy, David Hunt, Harvest House Publishers, Eugene, Oregon, 1995.

Jesus Vs. Jihad, Exposing the Conflict Between Christ and Islam, Marvin Yakos, Charisma House, Lake Mary FL. , 2001.

Leaving Islam—Apostates speak Out, Ibn Warraq, Prometheus Book, Amherst, NY, 2003.

Light and Shadow of Jihad—The Struggle for Truth, Ravi Zacharias, Multnomah Publishers, Sisters, OR, 2002.

Milestones, Sayyid Qutb, Mother Mosque Foundation, Cedar Rapids, IA, n.d.

Militant Islam Reaches America, Pipes, Daniel, W. W. Norton and Company, New York, 2003.

Reaching Muslims for Christ, William Saal, Moody Press, Chicago, 1991.

Secrets of the Koran, Don Richardson, Regal Books, Ventura, CA, 2003.

Share Your Faith With A Muslim, C.R. Marsh, Moody Press, Chicago, 1979.

The Bible and Islam, Bassam Madany, Back to God Hour, Palos Heights, IL, 1992.

The Complete Idiot's Guide to Understanding Islam, Yahiya Emerick, Alpha Books, Indianapolis, IN 2002.

The Crisis of Islam—Holy War and Unholy Terror, Bernard Lewis, The Modern Library, New York, 2003.

The Crucifixion of Christ: A Fact, Not Fiction—A Reply to: Crucifixion or Crucifiction, John Gilchrist, Muslim Friendship Ministries, Ontario, Canada, 1994.

The Decline and Fall of the Roman Empire, Edward Gibbon, Harcourt, Brace and Company, A One Volume Abridgment by D. M. Low, New York, 1960.

The Liberated Palestinian—The Anis Shorrosh Story, James and Marti Hefley, Victor books, Wheaton, IL, 1975.

The Muslims of America, Edited by Yvonne Yazbeck Haddad, Oxford University Press, New York, 1991.

The Oxford History of Islam, John Esposito, Oxford University Press, New York, 1999.

The Qur'an, Translated by Richard Bell, T. & T. Clark, Edinburg, 1937.

The Sword of the Prophet—Islam History, Theology, Impact on the World, Serge Trifkovic, Regina Orthodox Press, Boston, MA, 2002

Understanding Some Muslim Misunderstandings, Ernest Hahn, Fellowship of Faith for the Muslims, Toronto, ON, Canada, 2001.

Unveiling Islam—An Insider's Look at Muslim Life and Beliefs, Ergun and Emir Caner, Kregel Publications, Grand rapids, MI, 2002.

What you Need to Know About Islam and Muslims, George W. Braswell, Jr., Broadman and Holman Publishers, Nashville, TN, 2000.

Who Is This Allah? G.J.O. Moshay, Dorchester House Publications, Gerrard Cross, United Kingdom, 1995.

Why I Left Islam, Ibn Warraq, Prometheus Books, Amherst, NY, 1995.

Women in Islam, P. Newton and M. Rafiqui Haqq, The Berean Call, Bend, OR, 1995.

Subject Index

Person Index

GLOSSARY

Abbasid Caliphate at Baghdad from the eight to thirteenth century; claiming descent from Abbas, uncle of Mohammed.

Abu Bakr First Caliph in Mecca

Ali Son-in-law of the Prophet Mohammed; married the prophet's daughter, Fatima; first Imam of the Shi'ite sect, fourth Caliph.

Allah Arabic name for God.

Allahu Akbar "God is great."

Ayatollah Religious leader among the Sh'ites.

Bilal The first Muzzein (the person who calls Muslim to prayer).

Dar al-Harb "House of War"; areas of world unconquered by Islam.

Dar al-Islam "House of Islam"; territory under Muslim rule.

Dhimmi Minorities such as Christians and Jews under Muslim rule.

Din Religion and religious duties.

Fatwah A legal opinion given by a high religious leader.

Gabriel Angel that communicated the Koran to Mohammed.

Hadith Traditions; the recorded words, actions, and attitudes of the Prophet Mohammed.

Hafiz One who memorizes the Koran.

Hajj Pilgrimage to Mecca.

Hegira The flight of Mohammed and his followers to Medina. Beginning of Muslim calendar—A.D. September 20, 622.

Iblis Satan

Imam	Leader of the mosque.
Iman	Faith, belief, and doctrines of a religion.
Injil	The Gospel that was revealed to Jesus.
Jihad	Efforts to extend or defend the faith of Islam.
Kabah	"Cube"; the house of pilgrimage in Mecca.
Kafir	Infidel; non-believer.
Khadijah	First wife of Mohammed.
Khalifa	Caliph; successor of Mohammed.
Madrasa	Islamic religious school.
Mahdi	al-Mahdi; the guided one; like a Messiah.
Masjid	Mosque; where Muslims congregate to pray.
Mecca	Birthplace of Mohammed, site of the Kabah, destination of the pilgrimage.
Medina	Arabian city that welcomed Mohammed; location of his tomb.
Mufti	An Islamic leader qualified to issue a "fatwah."
Muslim	One who submits to Allah and confesses Mohammed to be His prophet.
Qur'an	The holy book of Islam; "recitations."
Quraysh	Mohammed's tribe in Arabia.
Ramadan	Ninth month of Muslim year; the month of the fast.
Rasul	Messenger or apostle; title of Mohammed.
Salat	Muslim prayer ritual.
Salaam	"Peace"; a salutation, greeting.
Sawm	Fasting
Shahada	Confession; "There is no god but Allah, and Mohammed is his prophet."

Shahid	A martyr.
Shari'a	Muslim rule or Muslim law.
Shi'ite	Minority Muslim community that accepted Ali as the successor of Mohammed.
Sheik	A religious leader; title of respect.
Shirk	Unpardonable sin of associating anything or any person with Allah.
Sunnah	Orthodoxy: the true path of Islam.
Sunni	Major Muslim community; claim to be orthodox Islam.
Sura	Chapter of the Koran; 114 surahs.
Umayyad	First dynasty of caliphs A.D. 661-750.
Wahhabi	Militant sect of Islam founded by al-Wahhab in Arabia A.D. 1703-92.
Zakat	Almsgiving

ORDERING INFORMATION

Telling the Truth!
by Gene Gurganus

Peril of Islam — Telling the Truth
by Gene Gurganus

Can be ordered from:
Truth Publishers
P.O. Box 1525
Taylors, SC 29687

1 copy	$10.00 postage paid
2 copies	$15.00 postage paid
5 copies	$30.00 postage paid
10 copies	$50.00 postage paid

Other Books by Gene Gurganus From Truth Publishers

*Perspectives on Evangelism
— Encouraging Effective Evangelism*
1 copy $15.00 postage paid

Preparing for the Conflict — Instructions from Peter
1 copy $10.00 postage paid

*Investing for Eternity — An Affirmation of the Faith
Promise Program for the Local Church*
1 copy $10.00 postage paid

The Great Omission — Fruit that Remains
1 copy $5.00 postage paid

Challenge of Islam (pamphlet)
1 copy $.50 postage paid
25 copies $5.00 postage paid
50 copies $10.00 postage paid
100 copies $15.00 postage paid